T&T CLARK STUDY GUIDES TO THE OLD TESTAMENT

JOSHUA

Series Editor
Adrian Curtis, University of Manchester, UK
Published in Association with the Society for Old Testament Study

T0331565

JOSHUA

An Introduction and Study Guide
Crossing Divides

By
James Gordon McConville

Bloomsbury T&T Clark
An imprint of Bloomsbury Publishing Plc

B L O O M S B U R Y
LONDON · OXFORD · NEW YORK · NEW DELHI · SYDNEY

Bloomsbury T&T Clark

An imprint of Bloomsbury Publishing Plc

Imprint previously known as T&T Clark

50 Bedford Square
London
WC1B 3DP
UK

1385 Broadway
New York
NY 10018
USA

www.bloomsbury.com

**BLOOMSBURY, T&T CLARK and the Diana logo are trademarks of
Bloomsbury Publishing Plc**

First published 2013. This edition published 2017

British Library Cataloguing-in-Publication Data
A catalogue record for this book is available from the British Library.

ISBN: PB: 978-0-5676-7097-7
ePDF: 978-0-5676-7098-4
ePub: 978-0-5676-7099-1

Library of Congress Cataloging-in-Publication Data
A catalog record for this book is available from the Library of Congress.

Series: T&T Clark Study Guides to the New Testament, volume 6

Cover design: clareturner.co.uk

Typeset by Newgen Knowledge Works (P) Ltd., Chennai, India

CONTENTS

PREFACE

I am grateful to Adrian Curtis for inviting me to contribute this volume on Joshua in the Phoenix Old Testament Guides series and so to replace his own excellent original! I have found it an ideal 'Guide' as I have prepared this one and have no doubt that it has plenty of shelf-life left in it. I hope the present volume may complement it in some ways.

I have struggled with Joshua in print a number of times, acutely aware of the difficulties and dangers it presents for some believing communities. For that reason, I have concluded the volume with a chapter on its impact in various times and places, culminating in a consideration of the conflict in Israel-Palestine. On this topic, I have benefited from conversations with many people on Joshua, both Old Testament scholars and others who are passionately interested in the interpretation of the Bible. Of these I might mention Charles and Anne Clayton, who introduced me to the work of Sabeel. I would like to dedicate the book to them, to Naim Ateek and to Sabeel.

ABBREVIATIONS

BEATAJ	Beiträge zur Erforschung des Alten Testaments und des antiken Judentums
BETL	Bibliotheca ephemeridum theologicarum lovaniensium
BZAW	Beihefte zur *Zeitschrift für die alttestamentliche Wissenschaft*
CBQ	*Catholic Biblical Quarterly*
FAT	Forschungen zum Alten Testament
IDB	George Arthur Buttrick (ed.), *The Interpreter's Dictionary of the Bible* (4 vols.; Nashville, TN: Abingdon Press, 1962)
JBL	*Journal of Biblical Literature*
JSOT	*Journal for the Study of the Old Testament*
JSOTSup	*Journal for the Study of the Old Testament*, Supplement Series
JTISup	*Journal of Theological Interpretation*, Supplement Series
LCBI	Literary Currents in Biblical Interpretation
NEAEHL	New Encyclopaedia of Archaeological Excavations in the Holy Land
NIBC	New International Biblical Commentary
ÖBS	Österreichische biblische Studien
OBT	Overtures to Biblical Theology
OTG	Old Testament Guides
SBLSymS	Society of Biblical Literature Symposium Series
SBTS	Sources for Biblical and Theological Study
SHS	Scripture and Hermeneutics Series
ThPQ	*Theologisch-praktische Quartalschrift*
VTSup	*Vetus Testamentum*, Supplement Series
WMANT	Wissenschaftliche Monographien zum Alten und Neuen Testament
ZAW	*Zeitschrift für die alttestamentliche Wissenschaft*

R.G. Boling and G.E. Wright (Anchor Bible; Garden City, NY: Doubleday, 1982). Older standard critical commentary, with strengths in history, geography and archaeology. Detailed textual notes.

Trent C. Butler, *Joshua* (Word Biblical Commentary; Waco, TX: Word Books, 1983). One of the early Word Commentaries, with that series' strengths on the text and bibliographies, though these are now a little dated. Combines a redaction-critical approach with a theological understanding of Scripture as God's word.

Jerome F.D. Creach, *Joshua* (Interpretation; Louisville, KY: John Knox Press, 2003). The Interpretation Commentary offers scholarly exegesis and theological interpretation, with a special eye on resourcing preaching and teaching. Creach gives sensitive exegesis and pays attention to the text both as history and as theology.

L. Daniel Hawk, *Joshua* (Berit Olam; Collegeville, MI: Liturgical Press, 2000). An influential recent commentary on Joshua, particularly sensitive to its literary character. Shows that the book's meaning, or 'ultimate semantic authority' (Bakhtin), is not identical to the meaning of individual utterances within it. Shows that Joshua challenges notions of what it might mean for Israel to be 'elect'.

Richard Hess, *Joshua* (Tyndale Old Testament Commentaries; Leicester: IVP, 1996). A conservative commentary in the Tyndale series. Gives quite a detailed treatment of the text and has an emphasis on matters of history, archaeology and the ancient Near Eastern context.

David M. Howard, Jr, *Joshua* (New American Commentary; Nashville, TN: Broadman and Holman, 1998). A conservative evangelical commentary that aims to do a theological exposition of the text. Deals with textual and historical issues.

J.G. McConville and S.N. Williams, *Joshua* (Two Horizons; Grand Rapids: Eerdmans, 2010). Offers a concise exegesis (McConville), together with treatments of theological topics (Williams) and some dialogue between the authors on matters of interpretation, especially history and theology.

Richard D. Nelson, *Joshua* (Old Testament Library; Louisville, KY: Westminster John Knox Press, 1997). Standard modern critical commentary. Very strong on the text of Joshua and on exegesis. Accounts for various stages of the composition of the book, but is also sensitive to 'synchronic' reading, and theological issues.

P. Pitkänen, *Joshua* (Apollos Old Testament Commentary; Leicester: Apollos, 2010). Recent substantial addition to the Apollos series. Conservative on dating Joshua, with a strong focus on historical and archaeological data. Gives attention to theological interpretation and has an unexpected application to modern Israel.

Hartmut N. Rösel, *Joshua* (Historical Commentary on the Old Testament; Leuven: Peeters, 2011). The Historical Commentary on the Old Testament is produced mainly by Continental scholars. It aims to represent the various stages in the interpretative process, including historical criticism, history of interpretation and exposition of the final text. Rösel is a good reference point for much recent scholarship on Joshua.

In German:

Volkmar Fritz, *Das Buch Josua* (Handbuch zum Alten Testament, 1/7; Tübingen: Mohr–Siebeck, 1994).

M. Görg, *Josua* (Die Neuer Echter Bible; Würzburg: Echter Verlag, 1991).

Ernst Axel Knauf, *Josua* (Zürcher Bibelkommentare; Zürich; Theologischer Verlag, 2008).

Joshua in the Canon

The book of Joshua is the sixth book of the canon of the Old Testament or Hebrew Bible. It therefore follows the Pentateuch, or the Five Books of Moses. Those books take the biblical story from the creation to the formation of the people of Israel, their covenant with Yahweh their God, and the death of their first great leader, Moses, who now finds a successor in Joshua. Joshua may be said to complete that story, with its culmination in Israel's occupation of land. It also stands at the head of the Historical Books of the Old Testament (Joshua–Kings), also known in the Hebrew canon as the Former Prophets (where the book of Ruth is excluded, being assigned there to the Writings).

Text

The book of Joshua, as it is known in English versions of the Bible, is a translation of the text on which the standard edition of the Hebrew Bible is based, namely the Leningrad Codex, dating from c. 1000 CE. This text is an example of the so-called Masoretic Text (MT), a form of the Hebrew Scriptures produced by scholars known as the Masoretes, who copied them during the first millennium CE, and added vowel pointing and certain directions for reading. The book of Joshua also exists in the pre-Christian Greek translation known as the Septuagint (LXX). In Old Testament studies, the LXX is taken as an important additional witness to the best or original text and it is not uncommon for scholars to correct the MT reading of a text or passage in favour of the LXX. In Joshua, MT is generally regarded as more reliable and commentators tend to prefer it, correcting from LXX occasionally. However, Nelson thinks that LXX, which is five percent shorter, witnesses to a Hebrew text at least equal in value to that of MT (Nelson 1997: 22). In a few cases, LXX evidently preserves a better text. Rösel cites the text following Josh. 15.59, where LXX has a description of a complete district of Judah omitted in MT, and also the Levitical cities of Reuben (Josh. 21.36-37), where cities missing in MT, but contained in LXX, are also found in the Hebrew of 1 Chron. 6.63-64 (Rösel 2011: 21). Nelson regards both

MT and LXX as 'expansionist', compared with a hypothetical original (p. 23). LXX has given to the history of interpretation the name *Iēsous* for Joshua, with its suggestive echo of the name of Jesus, a 'deliverer' in a different New Testament idiom.

There are also fragments of Joshua in Hebrew found at Qumran (4QJosh[a] and 4QJosh[b] = 4Q47 and 4Q48), but these have not yet had a decisive influence on the question of the best text.

What Is Joshua?

The book of Joshua is the memorable story of how a people crosses a river and becomes a nation in a land that is called by its own name. As such, it has left a deep impression on the public mind, wherever this has been formed by knowledge of the biblical narrative. The crossing of a river is a potent image of decisive progress and new opportunity. So Caesar's crossing of the Rubicon has also entered the common memory as a metaphor for irrevocable decision. Israel crossed the Jordan after a period of hesitation, delay and setback and a new life now lay before them. The image even found a place in Christian piety as a metaphor for the passage through death to life beyond the grave as in a verse of William Williams's well-known hymn, *Guide me, O thou Great Jehovah*:

> When I tread the verge of Jordan
> Bid my anxious fears subside.
> Death of death and hell's destruction
> Land me safe on Canaan's side.

A second iconic image follows immediately from the crossing of Jordan, namely the miraculous victory of the people of Israel over the fortified city of Jericho, whose walls famously fell down when the Israelites marched round it and sounded the *šôp̄ār* trumpet. The event is a favourite of story-book and song, as in the well-known Spiritual:

> Joshua fit de battle of Jericho,
> Jericho, Jericho,
> Joshua fit de battle of Jericho
> And de walls came tumblin' down.

So the people of Israel encounters more than the physical feature of a fairly modest river on their march, but deep hostility to their project, in the form of organized human power. That power is symbolized by Jericho and will take new forms as Israel progresses inexorably through the land.

In these two moments, both occurring in the early phase of the narra-tive (Josh. 3–6), we meet the profound challenge the book presents to the reader. Part of this challenge is its capacity to touch deep chords of human aspiration. There are aspirations about human identity, destiny and belonging in a place, which have lent the book an enduring appeal in the minds of quite disparate peoples throughout history. The notion of nationhood in the Christianized world arguably owes an enormous debt to the narrative of Israel, a people united in a noble purpose and fulfilling its destiny in the possession of land. The loyalty of people to their nation and a sense of shared values can be the seed-bed of courage and virtue. But the hard question is how such aspirations can be met within the context of a wider vision for the good of all peoples, a vision that readers of the Bible might be expected to share. Joshua's narrative of the violent dispossession of the Canaanites by Israel under the empowering hand of God resembles all too forcefully for many readers the horrors of 'ethnic cleansing' in many instances, down to our own day. Is there a way to read Joshua that does not lead to such things?

We will return to the question of uses and abuses of the book of Joshua later. For now, we may note two points. First, at the outset of the project, Joshua is charged to keep the 'law', the Torah of Yahweh (Josh. 1.6-8) and, at the end of the book, the people as a whole re-commit themselves to keep the covenant with Yahweh, made first at Mt Sinai (as told in the book of Exodus), the Torah being at its heart (Josh. 24). The Torah, at least as read by Israel's prophets, would, in the end, define the destiny of Israel in a way that is incompatible with nationalistic triumphalism.

Second, we recall also from the book of Exodus, that the story of Israel's possession of land began with their deliverance from slavery under the tyranny of Egypt. Yahweh delivered them from oppression at the hands of a power that subjected people absolutely to its own self-serving interests. This was antithetical to the kind of freedom that was to be Israel's destiny and which was enshrined in the Torah. In the image of the fall of Jericho, much depends on who the real oppressor is deemed to be. The singers of the Spiritual had no doubt how to read that.

The Study of Joshua

In the present volume, we will consider the important aspects of the study of the book. We begin with an outline of its narrative and contents (Chapter 1) in order to provide a basis for what follows. In Chapter 2, we consider the traditional literary criticism of the book, addressing matters of dating, sources and composition. We then turn, in Chapter 3, to an approach to the book as a work of literature. This pays attention not to the history of composition, but to the literary form of the book as it stands (essentially based on MT). The different approaches in Chapters 2 and 3 are compared for the effect they have respectively on the book's meaning. In Chapter 4, we consider questions of genre, asking especially whether it is properly regarded as history, and considering evidence for that, or whether it is really something else. Chapter 5 examines the theology of the book, an essential aspect of its study, since it claims to speak about God. Finally (Chapter 6), we consider the use that has been made of Joshua by believing communities, with special attention to its role in the conflicted politics of Israel-Palestine and ask how it might have a useful function in such situations.

The volume does not refer exclusively to one English version of the Bible. Where the author's own translation is not used, the Bible version used will be identified.

1

OUTLINE

Joshua is roughly a book of two halves, telling first how the promised land was occupied by Israel (chaps. 1–12), then how it was settled by being distributed among the tribes (chaps. 13–21). There are three further chapters, at the end of the book, in which the relationship of the Transjordanian tribes to the larger part of Israel west of the Jordan is settled (chap. 22) and, in two farewell discourses of Joshua, the covenant with Yahweh is reaffirmed (chaps. 23–24).

Joshua 1–12: 'Crossing' and Conquest

The story of the conquest has a long preamble, which might be called ground-clearing, or better 'crossing', the first encounter with Canaanites, in Jericho, coming only in chap. 6. Chapters 1–12, therefore, may be sub-divided. In 1.1–5.12, we read of the preparations to cross the Jordan into the land and the crossing itself. And in 5.13–12.24 are found actual accounts of battle and conquest.

1.1–5.12: Crossing

The book opens (1.1-9) with God's command to Joshua to cross the Jordan at the head of the people, together with exhortations to him to be courageous and to adhere faithfully to the law given by Moses (1.7). This law (Torah), or 'book of the law', is that which the reader of the Pentateuchal narrative has met already in Deuteronomy, where it is the deposit of the words spoken by Moses in that book (Deut. 28.58, 61). So the beginning of Joshua is also a middle, since it presents itself as coming after events previously narrated. The charge to Joshua points back to texts that introduce him in various ways, as the servant of Moses and as the one commissioned to lead Israel after Moses' death (Exod. 17.8-16; Num. 27.12-23; Deut. 1.37-38; 3.21-28; 31.1-23; 34.9). Joshua 1.1-9 takes an explicit lead from Deut. 31.7-13 where Moses charges Joshua in words similar to God's words here. Also taken as read is the promise of the land, made ages before to the ancestors of Israel (Deut. 1.8). The description of its extent makes a bracket between the beginning of Joshua and the end of Deuteronomy (Deut. 34.1-4) and harks back to promises recorded in Genesis (Gen. 12.1-3; 15.18-21). The opening of the book, therefore, signals that an expected time has come, a new era in which the person of Joshua would play the leading part and in which Israel would enter its God-given possession.

The preamble moves on to settle the important question of land east of the Jordan already occupied by several Israelite tribes – Reuben, Gad and the 'half-tribe' of Manasseh (1.10-18). In their cases, the process of conquest and settlement had already begun under Moses (Deut. 2.26–3.17) and they had no need to cross the Jordan. While the Jordan is highly symbolic of the passage of Israel from wilderness to land, it is not Israel's absolute border, for some of Israel lives beyond it to the east. In a sense, the Jordan marks the boundary between the periods of Moses and Joshua. One of the issues in the book will be how these two parts of the people relate to each other and constitute a unity (chap. 22). At this point, it is settled that the Transjordanians must assist their fellow-Israelites in the conquest of the west.

There is more ground-clearing in chap. 2, in which Jericho makes its first appearance in the narrative in the story of Rahab and the spies. It makes a link with 1.12-18 because Rahab declares that Jericho is in great terror because it has heard of Israel's successes in Transjordan (2.10-11). So here too the previous conquest of Transjordan by Moses, and indeed the exodus from Egypt before it, is seen as integral with the conquest of the west. In a sense, the story oddly delays the progress of Israel, for Israel already knew that the land had been given into their hands (2.24; cf. 1.2-5) and hardly needed a mission of spies to confirm it. But it functions in two ways: first, to identify Jericho as the primary objective of the military strike into the land and the key to its possession; and secondly, to explain why, after the conquest, there will still be some Canaanites alongside Israelites in the land. This too will be a recurring issue in the book (cf. chap. 9; 15. 63).

The crossing of the Jordan now follows, its importance signalled by the lengthy narrative devoted to it (chaps. 3–4) and the frequent repetition of the verb *'ābar* 'to cross' (21 times in chaps. 3–4). The journey takes the people from their camp at Shittim, east of the river (cf. Num. 25.1), to Gilgal on the west. Neither location is firmly identified, though Gilgal is speculatively identified with Khirbet el-Mefjir (Rösel 2011: 76; Fritz 1994: 49), lying between Jericho and the Jordan. More important, however, is the nature of the crossing, in which 'the ark of the covenant of Yahweh your God' (3.3), borne by the Levitical priests, plays a leading role. The ark is symbolic of God's presence with Israel and his guarantee that he will make good on his promise to be with Joshua and Israel as they cross into the land and confront the inhabitants who will be their enemies (3.10-11). It is also a sign (again) of continuity between Moses and Joshua (3.7), as indeed the miraculous parting of the waters of Jordan recalls that of the Reed Sea (3.16-17; 4.23-24; cf. Exodus 14–15). In this way the entry to Canaan forms bookends with the exodus in the grand narrative of the establishment of Israel as a people with a land. The event is marked by the setting up of twelve stones – variously, in the river itself (4.9) and in Gilgal (4.20) – to commemorate the coming of the twelve tribes to the land.

The peoples of the land are in fear of Israel, as Rahab had also testified (5.1; cf. 2.11). But there is yet more 'crossing' to be done, symbolically speaking, before the first battle (5.1-12). This consists in the act of circumcision of all the Israelites, a crucial marker of Israelite identity, which we now learn has been neglected during the wilderness years. The circumcising of Israel is connected with Gilgal, by way of an aetiological explanation of the meaning of the name, as a 'rolling away' of the shame of Egypt (5.9). (An 'aetiology' is an explanation of some familiar phenomenon by means of a narrative or saying about how it came about. Generally traditional rather than scientific explanations, they are often applied in the Old Testament to the names of people and places, as, for example, in Gen. 4.1, in order to bring out some perceived aspect of the person or place. In this case, the name of Gilgal has a resemblance to the verb meaning 'roll away', and this suggests to the author a link with its role in the story of deliverance in which it plays a part; cf. 4.19-24. Aetiologies in Joshua are linked with the feature of the book whereby certain phenomena are said to continue 'to this day', e.g. 4.9; 8.27.) Circumcision and Passover (5.10-12) are crucial parts of this narrative of separation. Passover once again looks back to the departure from Egypt and at the same time acts as a kind of 'Thanksgiving' on the part of these newly arrived travellers, a guarantee not only of victory, but of secure possession and the means of life.

5.13–12.24: Conquest

The pieces are now in place for the confrontation with Canaan. Before the action continues, there is a significant threshold moment when Joshua, unexpectedly, encounters a man with a drawn sword, who announces himself as 'the prince of the host of Yahweh' (5.13-15). The figure is reminiscent of 'the angel of the Lord', who, in other texts is, in effect, a manifestation of Yahweh (e.g. Judg. 13.21-22). And the incident is reminiscent of Moses' vision of Yahweh at Mt Horeb (Exod. 3.1-6), where also shoes are to be put off because the ground is 'holy'. The meaning is clear: the land is Yahweh's, as is the battle for it. And Israel's possession of it is of a piece with the covenant-making with Yahweh that began on the road from Egypt.

The account of the conquest of the land has both military and theological aspects. It charts a more or less systematic military progress from the destruction of the first important border city, Jericho, to the subjugation of the land, both north and south (11.23). The defeat of Jericho (chap. 6) is a key moment in the book. The repeated march around the city, led by priests blowing trumpets, the fall of the walls and the destruction of the people without a fight, demonstrate powerfully that it is Yahweh who gives the victory in this war. The Jericho episode introduces the concept of *ḥērem*, meaning a divine decree of total destruction (6.17-19). The command to subject Canaan to the *ḥērem* was given in Deut. 20.16-18, as part of commands about warfare, in which the *ḥērem* was to be applied only to the peoples of the land that God is giving Israel. (The concept was already applied to the Transjordanian victories in Deut. 2.34; 3.6.). In the case of Jericho, there are no exceptions to the command to leave nothing alive and to take no booty (6.18-19, contrast 8.2). This explains the long pause in the military progress in chap. 7, in which the family of Achan is found to have broken the terms of the *ḥērem* by taking spoils and, in consequence, they are subjected to the *ḥērem* themselves. The *ḥērem* has the symbolic meaning that what falls under it belongs to God and is put beyond the use of humans. Its application to an Israelite family curiously echoes its application to the Canaanite Jericho.

After Jericho (chap. 6) Joshua continues to make Gilgal his base camp, but the action moves into the hill-country lying above the Jordan to the west and the difficult routes through it that any invading army must control. This is the heart of the land, dividing the Jordan valley in the east from the lower hills and the fertile plain to the west and the Mediterranean coast. The key objectives here are Ai and Bethel (chap. 8, note 8.17) and, beyond these, the major city of Gibeon (chap. 9), which pre-empted Joshua's military attack by a trick. The territory from Jericho to Gibeon would comprise part of Benjamin in the tribal allocation to follow.

At this point, with the possession of the land only partly accomplished, Joshua leads a covenantal ceremony on Mt Ebal (8.30-35), in which an altar is built, sacrifices are made, and a copy of the Torah of Moses is written on the stones. Joshua and the people thus carry out a command recorded twice in Deuteronomy, at significant points in that book's structure (Deut. 11.29-30; 27.1-8), to perform such a ceremony upon entry into the land. Ebal is a prominent mountain close to its twin, Gerizim, in the vicinity of biblical Shechem (modern Nablus), in the heart of the land. This action is a symbolic marker, rather like planting a flag, laying claim to this land in the name of Yahweh and asserting that life in it will henceforth be lived under the banner of Yahweh's Torah.

From the position of strength now gained, Joshua can proceed to sub-due an alliance of kings, centred on Jerusalem, that band together against him to the south, in roughly what would become the territory of Judah (chap. 10). The narrative of conquest culminates with a northern campaign against another alliance, led by the king of Hazor, a city north of the Sea of Galilee, with a decisive battle against massed opposition at Merom (11.5), an unidentified location in Galilee. Finally, in chap. 12, there is a list of kings whom Israel defeated, recapitulating the progress of the conquest beginning with Moses' settlement of the Transjordanian tribes (12.2-6), then west of the Jordan, in the sequence of Joshua's victories in the hill-country, then the south and north.

While there is a clear logic to this military progression, it is striking that the progress from Jericho to Gibeon occupies much the greatest part of the account of it. This has led to the suggestion that this section of the book preserves memories of localized campaigns, in keeping with the prominence of Gilgal in the story (Curtis 1994: 22-25), and is based on different kinds of literary sources. The account of the battle for Ai, for example (chap. 8), is markedly different from that of Jericho because of its attention to the topography of the place and the tactics employed by Joshua to take it. Tour guides regularly demonstrate to their listeners just how the action proceeded based on the description here. The account of the northern campaign conspicuously highlights Hazor, but lacks the kind of specific detail that characterizes the narratives about Ai and, to some extent, the southern campaign. For this reason, the story of the northern war has been thought to have less historical substance, but rather to have been heavily influenced by a theological concept of total conquest, indebted to Deuteronomy (Nelson 1997: 151-52).

The theological aspects of the account of the conquest are clear. The victories of Joshua vindicate the promise of Yahweh that he would give the land to Israel and that they should not fear the opposition that would meet them in it (Deut. 1.21; Josh. 1.3-9; 11.6). The land is characterized as the land of the several peoples of Canaan (variously, six or seven) (12.8), recalling the command-promise in Deut. 7.1-3 that Israel should utterly destroy them (cf. Exod. 23.23-24). The story has borne out the confession of Rahab that the whole land was in dread of the advance of Israel (2.9-10; cf. 5.1; 9.1-2; 10.1-2). Even though, as we have seen, the account of the various campaigns is uneven and patchy, the victory is portrayed as absolute and complete. The list of kings in chap. 12, which contains a number who have not been previously mentioned, is intended to demonstrate not only the consistent and fierce opposition of the Canaanites to Israel, but also that the land was comprehensively taken. This is also the express conclusion of the narrative of the campaigns (11.23). The land as a whole has been brought under the rule of Yahweh and his Torah (8.30-35).

Finally, in the account of total victory, the defeat of the Anakim (11.21-22) strikes a powerful symbolic note. These were the giant race, also called the Nephilim, with their strange primaeval origins, who had struck special fear into the hearts of Israel at their first failed approach to the land (Num. 13.33; Deut. 1.28; 9.1-2; Gen. 6.1-4). The victory of Joshua in Canaan, therefore, is more than a tale of events in the life of historic Israel, but belongs within God's own subjugation of everything unruly and hostile in the created world (see also below on Josh. 18.1).

Joshua 13–21: Distribution of Land

13.1–19.51: Possession

In the logic of the book's structure, the land has now been taken and the next task is to decide who gets what. Most of chaps. 13–21 is devoted to allotting territory to the tribes and settling other issues of possession. There is a logical relationship between the divine gift of the land in the defeat of its inhabitants and the 'possession' of it (*l^erištāh*, 13.1, from the verb yrš 'possess'), which implies the activity of settlement as a task in itself. (The logical progression from defeating to possessing is well illustrated in the summarizing statement in 12.1; cf. 1.11; 15). This 'possession' can be seen as the unifying idea in chaps. 13–21, in which forms of the term yrš occur predominantly. The distinction between defeating in war and 'possessing' should not be overdrawn, however, since there is a connection between 'possessing' and 'dispossessing' and the verb yrš sometimes has to be translated in the latter way in chaps. 13–21 (e.g. in 13.12; 15.14; 19.47). This is when it appears in the 'hiphil' form, a grammatical function in Hebrew which can have the effect of altering a verb's basic meaning.

Even so, it is surprising when we read in 13.1 that Joshua is old and much of the land remains to be taken! This is in tension with 11.23-24, which had declared that he had taken the whole land and it had rest from enemies. And it sits oddly too with 23.1, where a reference to Joshua's great age introduces one of his farewell speeches to Israel. These incongruities are widely regarded as evidence of inconsistency in the book and of its complicated history of composition (Nelson 1997: 5; Creach 2003: 5-6; Satterthwaite 2007: 59-60).

The land yet to be taken is described in 13.2-6 and consists broadly of Philistine territory in the southern coastal plain and towards Egypt, an area in the far north around Lebanon and some in between (v. 4), which is hard to identify (Nelson 1997: 166). The passage may intend to say that land remained to be taken all the way from north to south and so corresponds to a perspective that can be found running through chaps. 13–17, namely that the victories over the inhabitants of the land were in fact partial and that the tribal allocations were only imperfectly possessed (e.g. 13.13; 14.12; 15.63; 16.10). This is a major factor in the interpretation of the book to which we shall return.

The preamble to chap. 13 closes with Joshua's mandate to distribute the land west of the Jordan to the nine and half tribes that have not already opted to settle east of the river (13.7). (In the arithmetic, Levi is left out of the count, but the number twelve is maintained by means of the division of Joseph into Ephraim and Manasseh; see 14.3-4). That settlement has been described several times in the biblical narrative to this point (Num. 32; Deut. 3.12-17; Josh. 1.12-18). The allocation of land to Reuben, Gad and the 'half-tribe' of Manasseh was described briefly in Deut. 3.12-17, but a more expanded form is now given, first in a broad sweep (13.8-14), then in greater detail (13.15-31), moving from south (Reuben) to north (half-Manasseh). The territory as a whole ran from the River Arnon (13.16), flowing into the Dead Sea from the east, to the southern end of the Sea of Galilee and extended east into the fertile lands of Gilead and Bashan.

The account is more than a chronicle of land-distribution; it contributes to an explanation of the character of Israel and its presence in the land. It does this in part by recalling history, especially Moses' victories in the region (13.12, 21). It also fills out the historical memory by recounting the death of the soothsayer Balaam (13.22), who had been hired by the Moabite king Balak to try to halt the progress of Israel (Num. 22–24). It notes, for the first time, that there were pockets of land not actually subdued by Israel and where the former population continued to live (13.13). And, finally, it re-asserts twice that the tribe of Levi, because of its priestly vocation on behalf of the whole nation, was to have no land-inheritance (13.14, 33; cf. Num. 18.21-24; Deut. 10.6-9; 18.1-2).

These theological and explanatory aspects of the account of land-possession continue in chap. 14, which yet again affirms the east-west divide in Israel and the special status of the Levites (14.1-5). Moreover, the distribution proper is further postponed in order to include a narrative about Caleb, who, alone with Joshua of those who had spied out the land, had believed God's promise and been spared to see its fulfilment (Num. 13.30-33; 14.6-10, 20-24). Caleb appears here as a wholly faithful Israelite and this cameo of him at the beginning of the story of the possession of the land east of Jordan is an expression of some of the key theological emphases of the book: the faith and courage to believe God's promise and the gifts of long life and well-being that ensue.

The account of the allocation of territory now stretches from 15.1 to 19.51. However, the structure of it is important to note because a disproportionately large amount of space is devoted to Judah (14.6a; 15.1-63) and the Joseph tribes, Ephraim and (half-)Manasseh (chaps. 16–17). The account for these tribes is separated from the remaining seven by the notice of an assembly of the whole people at Shiloh (18.1), followed by a new initiative of Joshua, in which he rebukes the seven tribes for being slow to go and take possession of the land (18.3; cf. 13.1) and commissions a small posse, drawn from each of the seven tribes, to survey it (18.4-6). The narrative from 18.11 to 19.48 then follows a distinctive pattern in which the drawing of seven lots for the seven tribes is systematically narrated. Even here, Benjamin forms something of an exception because it does not quite fall within the pattern (that is, its lot is not described as 'the first lot'; 18.11) and it, too, occupies more space, relatively speaking, than the remaining six. This structure of chaps. 15–19 seems to suggest the perspective and relative priorities of the book of Joshua. Judah's pre-eminence (as in other depictions of twelve-tribe Israel; cf. 1 Chron. 2.1–4.23) suggests that this perspective is Judah-centred, while relative prominence given to 'Joseph' and Benjamin may imply that the world in which the book came into being was one in which relations among these parts of historic Israel were important. Roughly, Judah and the Joseph tribes correspond to south and north in the sense in which that became decisive for the history of Israel in the division of the united monarchy of David and Solomon into two kingdoms (1 Kgs 12). 'Ephraim' became a standard sobriquet for the northern kingdom (frequently in Hosea, for example; see Hosea 5 *passim*). And Benjamin's history allied it at times with the north (as in the war between the house of Saul and that of David, 2 Sam. 2–4) and at times with the south (in effect, after the fall of the northern kingdom). The priority given to Judah and the Joseph-tribes, in particular, is matched by the relatively large size of their allotments. In the latter case, this is specifically addressed and justified in a narrative in which 'Joseph' complains that it has not enough land for its people (17.14-18).

Two further features should be noted. Firstly, there is no absolutely consistent pattern in the way in which the allocated lands are described. This is illustrated by the description of Judah's territory, which first proceeds by a boundary-description (15.1-12), goes on to tell a story about how Caleb gives his daughter, Achsah, in marriage to Othniel son of Kenaz because he took Kiriath-sepher in battle (15.13-19) and finally resumes the description of the territory, but now with a list of cities (15.20-63). This kind of variety is found throughout the present section of the book (chaps. 15–19). Descriptions of territory are interspersed with narratives that shed light on aspects of the life of Israel, as when Joseph demands more land (17.14-18) or when the northern migration of Dan is recorded (19.40-48; compare and contrast Judg. 18). As for the geographical data, there are certain unevennesses which suggest that the materials used here have had disparate origins and may come from different times. Cities assigned to Simeon in 19.2-8, for example, also appear in Judah's list in 15.26-32. The note in 19.9 sheds light on this, as evidence that Simeon, over time, simply lost its identity and merged with Judah. There are also overlaps between Judah and both Benjamin and Dan (Hess 1996: 246-47), again suggesting shifts over time in tribal boundaries. It is sometimes thought that city-lists and boundary-lists had disparate origins, perhaps as administrative lists (see Butler 1983: 184-85; see also Aharoni 1967: 76-82). One feature of the material is the term *gᵉbûl*, 'boundary', which is at home in the sections that actually document boundaries (as in 15.1-12), but which also appears in material that is not really border-description, but rather city-list (where *gᵉbûl*, has to be taken in the sense of 'territory'; Nelson 1997: 169, on 13.16; see also p. 219). In that case, the use of *gᵉbûl* would serve to lend uniformity to material of different sorts.

Finally, one special type of explanatory note has already been mentioned, namely where a tribe is said not to have been able to drive the Canaanites out of their allocated land (e.g. 13.13; 15.63; 16.10; 17.12-13). Most striking is the failure to take Jerusalem (15.63), which would be so important in the continuing story of Israel. The memories of Jerusalem in this early time are mixed, for in Judges 1.8 we read that it was taken by Judah, but in Josh. 18.28 it is assigned to Benjamin! The non-possession of the city dominates in the tradition, however, and it is left to King David, several generations after Joshua, finally to make it Israelite (2 Sam. 5.6-10). The notices about failure to possess the land fully amount to a motif, in line with the perspective in 13.1-7. It stresses the obligation on Israel to continue the task of possessing the land. And it is the contrasting counterpart of another feature of the narratives of land-distribution, namely the process of the 'lot', by which most of the land is allocated, and which stresses that the possession is the gift of God.

The Assembly at Shiloh

We have already noticed that the accounts of the land-distribution are put on pause at 18.1 where the whole people is said to assemble at Shiloh. The verse has two terms that apply to the formal gathering of the covenant people of Yahweh. One is *qāhāl*, here in verbal form, which in Deuteronomy denotes the formative assembly of the people at Sinai (cf. Deut. 5.22; 9.10). The other is *'ēdâ*, which does not occur in Deuteronomy, but rather in parts of the Pentateuch attributed to the Priestly writing (e.g. Num. 16.2). The meeting of the people at Shiloh is significant since, apart from the covenantal ceremony at Mt Ebal (Josh. 8.30-35), it is the first time in the book that they have gathered in one place other than at Gilgal. Shiloh is remembered

in the Old Testament as one of the early central worship places in Israel
(cf. Josh. 22; 1 Sam. 1–3; Jer. 7.12). The Tent of Meeting symbolizes the
presence of Yahweh with all Israel, since the time in the wilderness after the
exodus from Egypt (Exod. 33.7-11; cf. Deut. 31.14-15). This verse, then,
says much about the view of Israel projected by the book of Joshua and is
marked out as a significant moment. Remarkable here is the phrase 'the
land was subdued before them'. If this seems premature – since seven tribes
have still to enter into their inheritances – that is in keeping with the running tension in the narrative, between the perspective of total conquest and
that which leaves Israel with work still to be done. More significantly, the
phrase echoes the mandate given to the first humans at the creation in Gen.
1.28: 'Be fruitful, and multiply, and fill the earth, and subdue it…' Israel's
possession of its land, therefore, is seen as a fulfilment of the human mandate to exercise rule over the whole creation. (For literary-critical aspects of
this, see Auld 1998: 63-68; Brueggemann 1972; Blenkinsopp 1976).

20.1–21.45: Completing the Settlement

The provision for cities of refuge (20.1-9) was evidently an important part
of the organization of social space in Israel. Deuteronomy made a similar
provision at the end of its account of Moses' settlement of Transjordan (in
Deut. 4.41-43) and the book of Numbers does, too, near the end of its narrative of Israel's approach to the land prior to entry into it (Num. 35.6-15).
Common to these provisions is the number six, three on either side of the
Jordan. Joshua 20.7-9 repeats the three set aside by Moses for Transjordan
(Bezer, Ramoth, Golan) and names three in the west (Kedesh, Shechem
and Kiriath-arba). Deuteronomy appears to allow for the possibility of a
further three in the west, if necessary (19.4-10). These provisions not only
give an insight into ancient legal practices (cf. Exod. 21.12-13), but also
attend to the question, following the allocation of land, how responsibility
for applying the Torah would be borne by respective authorities in their
territories.

   The principle that the tribe of Levi, alone among the twelve, would have
no territorial inheritance has by now been well established (Josh. 13.14, 33;
14.4; cf. Deut. 10.6-9; 18.1-8). Instead, they would have cities and grazing
lands within each territory. Accordingly, Joshua 21 now presents a record
of these cities by tribe, a total of forty-eight (v. 41), including the six cities
of refuge. (A similar structure is recorded more briefly in Num. 35.1-8.)
The Levites' 'inheritance' is variously said to be the 'offerings by fire' (Josh.
13.14) and Yahweh himself (Deut. 10.9). But this does not mean they are
deprived of the means of life. Rather, they have a presence in the whole
land, as a sign that it is in its entirety the gift of Yahweh to Israel. With the

list of Levitical cities, and the presumed occupation of them, the settlement of the tribes in their lands may be said to be complete. Here, as elsewhere, a certain precedence is given to Judah-Simeon-Benjamin, in which thirteen cities are allocated to the Aaronic branch of the tribe of Levi (21.4). The special priestly privilege of Aaron within the tribe of Levi is found in Numbers (Num. 3–4; 18), but in most accounts not in Deuteronomy, placing this part of Joshua close to the concept of the Priestly literature. The scheme of four cities per tribe, which is not quite maintained (vv. 19, 32), may suggest that an original core list was expanded artificially (see Nelson 1997: 238-39; Ben Zvi 1992).

Joshua 22–24: Prospects

The final three chapters return to the key premise of the book that Israel is to worship the one God, Yahweh, in the land given to them.

In chap. 22, the question of the Transjordanian tribes recurs once more, as if to deal finally with a troublesome problem and suggesting that it must have been a hot issue for the audience of the book. Joshua charges them to remain faithful to Yahweh and his Torah (vv. 1-9). It is intriguing that in v. 9 we read that the Transjordanians 'part from the people of Israel at Shiloh' to go to 'their own land'. This distinction has been implied throughout the book (cf. 5.12; 14.1; 21.2), but it is highlighted here, uniquely, by the designation of Transjordan, in contrast to 'the land of Canaan', as 'the land of Gilead' (cf. Num. 32.29-30; in 17.5-6, 'the land of Gilead' is more restricted, part of the territory of half-Manasseh, as in 13.11; 21.38). Were the Transjordanians fully Israelite like their kin to the west? The issue comes to a head when they erect a great altar by the Jordan, an act which almost leads to war, but ends with the mutual acceptance that it was meant not as an emblem of division, but on the contrary, as a memorial of their unity with Israel by virtue of their participation in worship at Shiloh (22.21-34). The episode is the final act in the narrative of the possession of the promised land. It leaves ajar the question of the proper extent of the land of Israel, but it insists firmly on the unity of the people.

There are two further acts at the conclusion of the book: a farewell discourse by Joshua (chap. 23) and a covenant renewal by the tribes at Shechem (chap. 24).

The speech in chap. 23 is from a leader who is near the end of his life (23.14), similar in function to Moses' Song (Deut. 32), and a charge to Israel to continue to keep faithful to Yahweh and his Torah, in order to continue to enjoy the gift of the land. It contains a number of typically 'Deuteronomic' features. It forms a 'bookend' with Joshua 1, with its command to obey 'the book of the law of Moses' (23. 6); it recalls the Shema, that basic command of Moses in Deuteronomy to love Yahweh and keep his commands (23.11; cf. Deut. 6.4-9); it has an echo of the Song of Moses (23.10; cf. Deut. 32.30); it repeats the prohibition both of foreign worship and of mixed marriage with the people of Canaan (23.7, 12; cf. Deut. 7.1-5) and it employs the blessing and the curse, a formal feature of ancient Near Eastern treaties also adopted by the rhetoric of Deuteronomy (23.15-16; cf. Deut. 28; 30.1). The force of this deployment of the rhetorical strategies of Deuteronomy is to put the possession of land perpetually in the balance; Israel has been given this land for now, but its possession of it depends entirely on its putting into practice of Yahweh's Torah there (23.16; cf. Deut. 4.25-26). The message is one that might have had force at any time in Israel's history.

The final chapter (chap. 24) forms, with chap. 23, a double finale to the book. Each involves an assembly of all Israel called by Joshua (23.2; 24.1), the first in an unspecified place, the second at Shechem. It is not clear how the two assemblies relate to each other. Shechem was close to Mt Ebal, where a covenant ceremony had already taken place (8.30-35). The passage features several formal elements of a treaty or covenant: a history of the relationship between the parties to it (vv. 2-13); general and specific conditions (respectively, they should serve Yahweh alone, vv. 14-15, and obey his 'statutes and ordinances', vv. 25-26); sanctions (v. 20); a written document containing the conditions, as evidence of the covenant (vv. 25-26). (For accounts of treaties and covenants, see Baltzer 1971; McCarthy 1981).

It has, however, its own distinctive form, based on dialogue between Joshua and the people (vv. 14-24). In this context, the moral challenge faced by Israel is put very starkly (v. 19; cf. v. 22 and echoes of the function of the Song of Moses again, Deut. 31.24-29). Joshua makes his own declaration that he and his 'house' will serve Yahweh (v. 15b), giving notice that this will be a touchstone of the unity and integrity of Israel. He 'retires' and retreats to his own 'inheritance' at Timnath-serah (v. 29; cf. 19.50). And he dies at the age of 110 years (symbolic of a great age and a fulfilled life, as with Joseph, Gen. 24–25). In a coda, the bones of Joseph himself are now brought from Egypt in fulfilment of his wish, tying the action of Joshua into the history of the people since patriarchal times. The final word concerns the death and burial of Eleazar, the Aaronite priest (24.33).

Issues Arising from the Outline

From the Outline just offered, it has emerged that one cannot simply tell the story of the book of Joshua without raising a number of questions about its nature along the way. These include its literary formation, its relation to the history of Israel and Judah, its genre and purpose and its theology. In the chapters that follow, we will consider each of these in turn. In a final chapter, we will also consider the question if and how a book that is predicated on the decision of God to grant a land to a particular people at the expense of others, by violent means, might be regarded as having a constructive meaning in the modern world and faith communities.

Bibliography

Aharoni, Y. *The Land of the Bible: A Historical Geography* (London: Burns & Oates, 1967 [original, Hebrew, 1962]).

Auld, A.G. *Joshua Retold: Synoptic Perspectives* (Edinburgh: T. & T. Clark, 1998).

Baltzer, K. *The Covenant Formulary in Old Testament, Jewish and Early Christian Writings* (trans. David E. Green; Oxford: Blackwell, 1971).

Ben-Zvi, E. 'The List of the Levitical Cities', *JSOT* 54 (1992), pp. 77-106.

Blenkinsopp, J. 'The Structure of P', *CBQ* 38 (1976), pp. 275-92.

Brueggemann, W. 'The Kerygma of the Priestly Writers', *ZAW* 84 (1972), pp. 397-413.

Curtis, Adrian H.W. *Joshua* (OTG; Sheffield: Sheffield Academic Press, 1994).

McCarthy, Dennis J. *Treaty and Covenant* (Analecta biblica; Rome: Pontifical Biblical Institute Press, 2nd edn, 1981).

Satterthwaite, Philip E., and J. Gordon McConville. *Exploring the Old Testament 2: The Historical Books* (London: SPCK/Downers Grove, IL: IVP, 2007).

2

JOSHUA IN LITERARY CRITICISM

The term 'literary-criticism' is traditionally used in Biblical Studies to describe the study of the process by which the biblical books were formed. It has also come to bear another meaning, namely their appraisal in terms of their literary properties, such as plot, character and the features of the writing, whether narrative or poetry. These are distinct, though related, kinds of enquiry. In this chapter we will consider literary criticism in the first sense of the term.

It is important to note at this point that there are divergent views about literary criticism. There is a lively 'conservative' scholarly tradition that differs markedly from the common critical approach to the Old Testament, and in relation to Joshua, takes it to have been composed close to the events it narrates (of the commentaries listed at the beginning of this volume, Howard, Hess and Pitkänen, with certain differences, fall within this class). These differences are philosophical and theological. That is, they relate to the understanding of what is entailed in a belief in the Bible as the Word of God for issues of composition and history of the text. In critical scholarship, the canons of ordinary historical and literary research are applied to biblical study, while conservative commentary tends to regard these as called into question by divine revelation, which is held to leave room for the extraordinary and the miraculous not only in God's acts in history, but in the process of the Bible's composition. It is not possible to address these philosophical differences here, but only to note their existence, and explain the position taken here. The present Guide follows a broadly critical approach and therefore attends in general more to the critical literature. But the conservative commentary is respected for its contribution to the exegesis of the texts. Those who read it will find alternative views and often direct responses to those expressed here. It should be said, finally, that the approach one chooses to adopt on this closely affects the kinds of use and interpretation of the book that are open to the reader. This should become clear as we proceed, and especially when we consider the interpretation and uses of the book of Joshua. (For approaches to the interpretation of Scripture, see Goldingay [1994]).

The Formation of the Book of Joshua

Our overview of the contents of Joshua in the preceding chapter showed that, while it can be re-told as a coherent story, it has features that suggest that it was not an entirely unified composition and may have come into being over time. Examples of this were as follows: there is a tension between the perspective of a total conquest (11.23) as against the view that much land remained to be taken (13.1); in two places Joshua is said to be 'old and advanced in years' (13.1; 23.1), the former declaring that he still has work to do, while the latter assumes the work is done and is a prelude to his farewell address to Israel. Partly on the basis of the preceding point, it has been supposed that chaps. 13–22 have a separate origin from chaps. 1–12 and have been placed into their position secondarily. This was the influential view of Martin Noth, still advocated by some (e.g. Nelson 1997), though not all (Fritz 1996: 4-6; Auld 1998). There were unevennesses in the narratives of conquest and distribution. In both chaps. 5–12 and 13–19, there is a disproportionate emphasis on the territory of what would become Judah and Benjamin and generally less on the north. This is reflected in the structure of chaps. 13–19, with its premature narrative peak at 18.1, where the tribes gather at Shiloh following the lengthy account of the possessions of Judah and the Joseph tribes, and its briefer and more formulaic description of the remaining tribes' possessions in 18.11–19.48. (Among these, Benjamin is relatively prominent, 18.11-27; the last six are dealt with entirely in chap. 19). This suggests a provenance in a period when the southern territory was a present reality while the concept of a twelve-tribe Israel occupying the full extent of the promised land was rather ideal.

The lists themselves have been thought to reflect times and conditions in Israel's history much later than Joshua. We noticed in the preceding chapter that certain cities appear in more than one list (see Hess 1996: 246-47). According to de Vos, in his lengthy study of the 'lot' of Judah, the roughly 120 places named after 15.21 did not exist in the time of Joshua, but mostly came into being at about the same time in the seventh century BCE, though there may be older material in Josh. 15.1-12 (de Vos 2003: 6). The lists' reflection of changing historical conditions is also indicated by the fact that certain place-names occur separately in lists of Judah and Benjamin. The lists are, in the end, literary compositions that, like the narratives, encapsulate theological points of view. One example of this is an extension of the notion of 'the lot' (gôrāl) to texts where this term may not originally have occurred. The Old Greek of 15.1; 16.1; 17.1 has 'territory', based on Hebrew gᵉbûl, which appears to correspond better to 18.5-10, where the instruction to cast lots is first made (Nelson 1997: 183). For de Vos, this suggests a conforming of the whole text to an interest in divine communication and 'order' that might be regarded as 'priestly'. He finds a tendency towards such an interest developing in the text and illustrated by 14.1, in which v. 1b is an expansion emphasizing priestly authority in the distribution of the possessions of Israel (de Vos 2003: 184-85; cf. 207-208).

Commentators on the book of Joshua, therefore, have come to consider each part of it in terms of the conditions in which it might have been written and for what purpose and are alert for signs of redactional activity that suggest it has passed through stages in its composition. The story of Rahab (Josh. 2), for example, may have existed independently in an early form, as a tale of how a clever woman outwits the authorities in her city and turns a dangerous situation to her advantage, before being expanded and incorporated into the narrative of Joshua. Certain marks of a process of development in the narrative have been observed, such as the difficulty of reconciling the 'three days' in Josh. 2.16, 22 with Josh. 1.11; 3.2 (Rösel 2011: 43-44; Nelson 1997: 41) and in the narrative relationship between the story and the account of the fall of Jericho in chap. 6, where there is no mention of the 'scarlet thread' that was to identify Rahab's house to the Israelites (2.18), nor to the fact that the house was in the walls (2.15) and, therefore, in the logic of chap. 6 would have fallen down (Nelson 1997: 41). Why in any case was espionage necessary when Jericho was to be miraculously overcome? (Rösel 2011: 44). In the present narrative, however, the story serves theological themes of the book of Joshua, most evidently in the language adopted by Rahab in 2.9-11, where she articulates the 'Deuteronomic' theology of the gift of the land to Israel, knows of the drying up of the Reed Sea at the exodus from Egypt and of Israel's victories over Sihon and Og in Transjordan on their approach to Canaan. She even employs Deuteronomic language and theology in this rehearsal of Israel's history (2.11b; cf. Deut. 4.39). Consequently, Nelson finds three levels of meaning in the story: as a tale told in Israel (remembering an act of Canaanite treachery that had helped them); as a story in an early form of the book of Joshua, telling of the terror of the Canaanites at the approach of Israel (e.g. vv. 9a, 10a, 11a, 24a), and finally in the 'Deuteronomistic' form of the book, now part of the larger narrative of the Deuteronomistic History (Deuteronomy–Kings). This last level sets the story into that framework, as when it recalls the victories in Transjordan (Deut. 2.26–3.17; Nelson 1997: 41; cf. Creach 2003: 31).

From these observations about both the narratives and the descriptions of the inherited territory, it is clear that modern scholarship plots the composition of Joshua against an underlying thesis about the development of the Old Testament literature. This in turn is pegged to an understanding of the changing historical conditions in which the book in its stages would have made sense. We will now look at this aspect of the book more closely.

Joshua: A Book?

The question of Joshua's formation may be approached by observing first the tension between its character as an individual book and the fact that it takes its place as one of a succession of books within a longer connected narrative. This longer narrative may provisionally be identified as Genesis to Kings, though as we shall see one should not make such an assumption prematurely.

That Joshua can be regarded as a book in its own right is clear from several factors. Chiefly, it is unified by the figure of Joshua. It covers the period between the death of Moses (Deut. 34.5-12) and Joshua's own death (Josh. 24.29-30). This corresponds to a distinct phase in the narrative of Israel's history, namely their entry to the land of Canaan and settlement there. Joshua is expressly presented as a successor to Moses in the bridge between the end of Deuteronomy (Deut. 34.9-12) and the beginning of Joshua (Josh. 1.1-2; cf. Deut. 31.1-8, 13-15) and the book ends with a cov-enant-renewal, in which Joshua appears as a kind of second Moses, mak-ing 'statutes and ordinances' which he writes in a book, and in the last act of his life, challenging the people prophetically to keep the covenant (Josh. 24.25-27; cf. Deut. 32). The narrative of Joshua is unified by its clear structure and its thematic focus on possession and settlement. In the longer story, therefore, it falls between the forty-year wanderings in the wilder-ness of Sinai following the exodus from Egypt (Exodus–Numbers) and the people's subsequent life in the land, which begins to be told in the book of Judges. A further unifying factor is its formal resemblance in important respects to an ancient 'conquest narrative' (Younger 1990). Finally, Joshua has distinctive features in relation to the literary character of the books that precede and follow. While the analysis of the book cannot avoid using the concepts 'Priestly' and 'Deuteronomic' (or 'Deuteronomistic'), which are major conceptual tools in the analysis of all the literature from Genesis to Kings, it will become clear that in Joshua these take on certain hues of their own. (The terms 'Priestly' and 'Deuteronomic' are commonly used in Old Testament studies to describe distinct sources or strands that are gen-erally thought to have fed into what we know as the Pentateuch. In classic source-theory, 'Priestly' and 'Deuteronomic' correspond to the 'P' and 'D' of the four sources JEDP. J and E stand respectively for 'Yahweh', or Jahweh, and Elohim, the names of God preferred by the earliest Pentateuchal sources. D and P are, broadly speaking, from the period just before the exile to the period after it. They are recognizable by features of both form and content. 'Priestly' designates literature that shows a pronounced interest in the times, places, personnel and rituals of worship, as in Exodus 25–40 and much of Leviticus, while 'Deuteronomic', or 'Deuteronomistic', implies some connection with the book of Deuteronomy, with its distinctive style and theology. The terms are also applied to Old Testament literature outside the Pentateuch that is thought to be influenced by these strands.)

Joshua, therefore, is a book in its own right and commentators sometimes elect to assert this strongly in their treatment of it (e.g. Rösel 2011: 1). Yet it is already clear that even its individuality can only be understood in relation to the books that precede and follow. The fundamental literary-critical datum in Joshua is the fact that it purports to tell of events at the very inception of Israel's history in the land, but sits in a literary bloc which stretches to the Babylonian exile, in which the land was lost. This last statement should be qualified because it applies properly to Joshua in the MT, and thus in the canon of the Hebrew Bible. In the LXX and in the Christian Old Testament, it stands within a bloc that runs as far as Nehemiah, or Esther, and so to a time beyond both exile and restoration (Dozeman *et al.* 2011). In either case, the story of Joshua's literary formation therefore becomes inseparable from that of its larger literary framework.

Pentateuch, Hexateuch, Deuteronomistic History

It is clear, in general terms, that Joshua continues the story begun in the Pentateuch, most obviously because it tells about the conquest of the land that has been promised since early in Genesis (Gen. 12.1-3), pursued through the wilderness wanderings (Exodus–Numbers) and expressed repeatedly in Deuteronomy's theology of gift. The links between Joshua and the preceding books can be documented in some detail. The conquest of the land is anticipated in Gen. 15.12-21; Exod. 3.17; 23.23-33 and Numbers 32–35. The last of these includes the rationale for the prohibition of the exodus generation, with the exception of Joshua and Caleb, entering the land (Num. 32.11-13), the Transjordanian settlement and the status of the eastern tribes, the stages of the journey from Egypt to Moab, the location of Moses' speeches in Deuteronomy and the camp from which the crossing of the Jordan was launched (Num. 33.1-49). It makes preparations for conquest and distribution of the land, the respective roles of Joshua and Eleazar (Numbers 34), and the provision of cities for the Levites and cities of refuge (Numbers 35). The covenantal ceremony in Josh. 8.30-35 is commanded in advance in Deut. 27.1-8. Finally, Joshua 24 makes explicit links with both Genesis and Exodus, when it rehearses the story of Israel from Abraham's origins in Mesopotamia (Josh. 24.2-3; cf. Gen. 11.27–12.3), and tells that the Israelites brought up the bones of Joseph from Egypt for burial in the promised land, according to Joseph's last wish (Josh. 24.32; cf. Gen. 50.25; Exod. 13.19).

In literary-critical terms, these observations have to be considered in relation to the composition of the Pentateuch and the books that follow it canonically. The Pentateuchal narrative is, in a sense, incomplete because it has no account of the promised conquest, but finishes with the death of Moses, still outside the land (Deuteronomy 34). The apparent completion of the story in Joshua has led some to the concept of a Hexateuch (a six-fold scroll, in contrast to the Pentateuch's five). This is usually attributed to Gerhard von Rad (von Rad 1938 [1966]: 1-78, but see also Driver 1892: 1-150; cf. Freedman, *IDB*). Today, it is common to speak of a 'Hexateuch redaction' (Dozeman 2011: 29-30; Knauf 2008: 20-21; Römer 2011: 29).

A 'Hexateuch', however, does not account for all of Joshua's literary relationships, for as we have seen, the book is also embedded in a narrative that runs through to Kings. There are a number of specific echoes of Joshua in the books that follow. Joshua's curse on anyone who would rebuild Jericho after its destruction (Josh. 6.36) is explicitly recalled in 1 Kgs 16.34, when Hiel of Bethlehem built it 'at the cost of" his two sons. The identification of Shiloh in Joshua as a meeting-place and worship centre for all the tribes (Josh. 18.1; 22) finds a correspondence in 1 Samuel 1–3 (cf. Judg. 21.19 and the 'Deuteronomistic' Jer. 7.12). Joshua's record of the failure to take Jerusalem from the Jebusites in pre-monarchical times is a prelude to the narrative of King David's success in doing so (Josh. 15.63; cf. 2 Sam. 5.6-10). More generally, Joshua's story of land-possession is balanced in the end by that of its loss and the departure of the people once again into a foreign land with new masters, the Babylonians (2 Kgs 25). Joshua makes a further bookend with Kings in its stress on the importance of Torah and covenant in relation to the tenure of the land. And finally, Joshua himself is often held to measure up to the ideal for a king in the law of Deut. 17.14-20 and also to foreshadow the pious King Josiah who renewed the covenant on the basis of a rediscovered Torah (2 Kgs 22–23; see Nelson 1981).

These connections are emphasized in the concept of the so-called Deuteronomistic History (DtrH), a theory attributed to Martin Noth (Noth 1943 [1981]), that ran counter to von Rad. Noth believed that the Historical Books (Joshua–Kings) were composed under the influence of a theology that was classically expressed in Deuteronomy. It was Deuteronomy that laid a heavy stress on Torah, as also on the worship of Yahweh alone, expressed in the distinctively Deuteronomic idea of Yahweh's choice of a single central sanctuary for his worship (as in Deut. 12). This idea is present in Joshua in relation to Shiloh and also in the phrase 'at the place which he would choose' in Josh. 9.27 (cf. Deut. 12.5). Accordingly, Noth saw Deuteronomy as the beginning of a major bloc of literature rather than the end and held

that the established documentary sources of the Pentateuch did not continue beyond the end of Numbers. This view traded, to an extent, on the
classical nineteenth-century literary-critical premise that Deuteronomy
broadly represented a distinct Pentateuchal source, the 'D' of JEDP (see
note on this above: *Joshua: A Book?*).

In this theory, Joshua becomes the first book in a series that tells the
story of Israel in the light of Deuteronomic theology. For Noth, Joshua
1–12 consisted of pre-Deuteronomistic material, not deriving from the old
Pentateuchal sources JE, but from a 'collector' (German '*Sammler*'), which
had been subjected to re-working from a Deuteronomistic point of view.
Variations of this theory are maintained in modern commentary. Nelson
holds essentially to Noth's analysis of Joshua 1–12 (Nelson 1997: 5-9). Fritz
also considers Joshua 1–12 to be Deuteronomistic, but unlike Noth he finds
no evidence of a written source prior to a Deuteronomistic redaction. For
Fritz, all accounts of conquest presuppose the concept of a united Israel and
of united military action, which cannot predate the monarchy. The oral stories are 'saga'; only the place-names are 'historical' (Fritz 1994: 5). All other
narratives come from the author of what he calls the *Grundschicht* (or 'basic
layer', p. 6). This 'basic layer' in chaps. 1–12 comes from the Deuteronomist
and it was then reworked in two redactional layers; one Deuteronomistic
(RedD), the other Priestly (RedP; Fritz 1994: 4–5). In adopting this model,
Fritz follows the form of Deuteronomistic theory associated with R. Smend
(Smend 1971 [2000]).

The Deuteronomistic theory is flexible enough, with its underlying
notion of inherited material re-worked by a succession of redactors, to
accommodate the variety of kinds of writing that make up the historical
books. Where there are tensions or discrepancies, these can be attributed
to different redactional layers or pressures from older material. One such
discrepancy, well-known in Joshua studies, is the unexpected sequence
from the end of Joshua to the beginning of Judges, where, after the death
of Joshua, the Israelites are still in the position of having to 'fight against
the Canaanites' for their allotted land (Judg. 1.1-4). (It will be recalled
that a similar note is also struck in parts of Joshua and this was seen as a
sign of internal inconsistency there.) Another somewhat surprising point
in 'DtrH' is the omission of Joshua from 1 Sam. 12.6-11, where Samuel
recalls past heroes in a story that leads from the exodus to the occupation
of the land.

The theories of a Hexateuch and of a Deuteronomistic History were
strictly incompatible. Initially, they were harmonized in scholarship by the
assumption that an old Pentateuchal account (or accounts) of the conquest had been lost or suppressed and was/were replaced by what is now
found in Joshua (see Schmid 2011). This was intended to explain why the

Pentateuchal narrative had no 'ending', while at the same time its story was continued in a separate work that began in Deuteronomy.

In modern scholarship, a new synthesis has emerged, in which the major feature is the belief that a Dtr layer or layers run/s through the Pentateuch. Such a redaction explains, for example, why Abraham in Genesis can be depicted as having kept the 'commandments and statutes and laws', in terms very similar to Deuteronomy (Gen. 26.5; Schmid 2011: 23). Schmid documents this tendency in both English and German scholarship, citing E. Blum and John Van Seters, among others, as key influences (Schmid 2011: 18-23) and Blenkinsopp's *Introduction* (Blenkinsopp 1992) as an illustration that this has now entered the textbooks. The result is that it has become harder to make a clear distinction between the Pentateuch and DtrH. (This explains the notion of 'Farewell to the Yahwist'; Dozeman and Schmid 2006.) In fact, it has become common to speak now of a 'primary history' (already coined by Freedman 1962) or an Enneateuch (that is, nine scrolls) when referring to Genesis–Kings as a single bloc. (The nine are composed of the five books of the Pentateuch plus Joshua, Judges, Samuel and Kings. Samuel and Kings count as one each, not two, in accordance with the reckoning of ancient sources. Ruth does not occur in this bloc in the Hebrew canon, but rather in the division known as the Writings).

In a further departure from classical criticism, this extension of the Dtr theory also supposes that it has accommodated to Priestly concerns (Schmid 2011: 19). This then becomes a model for Joshua, notably chaps. 13–24, where scholars often note the presence of Priestly language and ideas yet do not attribute these directly to the Pentateuchal Priestly narrative source (P). The new model allows Joshua 13–24 to be regarded as integral to the concept of Joshua, whereas for Noth it had been a late insertion into a Dtr work (Fritz 1994: 7; Auld 1980: 52-71). This is because Joshua can now be seen as subject to a concept that has brought together language and ideas from both Dtr and Priestly milieux. Knauf's 'Hexateuch redaction' manifests precisely this and can express 'D'-theology in 'P'-language (Num. 31) and 'P'-theology in 'D'-language (Deut. 9–11; Knauf 2008: 21)!

In modern redaction-critical theory, the literature is often thought to have undergone an exceedingly complicated process of composition, reflecting ever-changing circumstances and theological controversies. Scribes and scholars worked tirelessly on texts, first around the palace, then the temple (Knauf 2008: 16-17). In the end, he believes, Priestly 'pragmatists' in Yehud (the post-exilic Persian province of Judah, as portrayed in Ezra–Nehemiah), prevailed over Deuteronomic 'Utopians' (Knauf 2008: 20-21). By this he means that the religious leadership settled for existence as a cultic community, with Torah becoming a fixed canon. This is reflected in Joshua in the picture of Israel as an organized cultic community in Joshua 3–4; 6, and in the land-distribution in chaps. 14–17.

In fact, it is difficult to determine an end-point to such activity. In recent criticism, as in older approaches, it remains a question whether Joshua is an ending or a beginning. One modern account of Genesis–Kings in redactional terms makes Joshua 24 a kind of hinge, in which Genesis–Joshua expresses a 'salvation-history' (*Heilsgeschichte*), while Judges–Kings goes into reverse and narrates a 'judgment-history' (literally an '*un*salvation-history', *Unheilsgeschichte*; Schmid 1999). Others have seen Joshua 24 as simply forming a conclusion to the Hexateuch (see Dozeman 2011: 186). Some have attempted to describe a series of redactions in the Enneateuch and Joshua in particular (e.g. Knauf 2008: 17-22). But such description may be finally elusive.

The open-ended nature of the compositional process in Joshua may be seen in the divergent editorial activity in the MT and LXX forms of the book, which Dozeman considers 'part of the history of composition' (Dozeman 2011: 199). He finds that Joshua MT places a higher value on the Torah-Moses connection, while LXX highlights the promise of land and minimizes the difference between Joshua and Judges on the people's faithfulness. Joshua MT sits within the tripartite canon of the Hebrew Bible, where Joshua is strongly linked with Deuteronomy, Torah and Moses, though a canonical separation is maintained between the books. The book of Joshua becomes, in this case, the first of the Former Prophets, Joshua himself being the successor to the prophet Moses, leading the people in faithful covenant keeping. In LXX, in contrast, the book finishes with the report that Israel worshipped 'Ashtaroth and the gods of the nations' and that God gave them into the hands of Eglon, King of Moab (Josh. 24.33b; cf. Judg. 3.12-30). Here the book of Joshua leads more naturally into Judges and the Historical Books and so forms part of that canonical division, stretching to Chronicles, which is familiar in the traditional Christian form of the Bible (Dozeman 2011: 205-09). This leads him to the conclusion that these forms of editorial activity create 'an intertext, by which the book of Joshua is integrated editorially within an evolving collection of books' (Dozeman 2011: 208). The position of Joshua in its canonical context is thus contested to the end.

Bibliography

Auld, A.G. *Joshua, Moses and the Land: Tetrateuch, Pentateuch, Hexateuch in a Generation since 1938* (Edinburgh: T. & T. Clark, 1980).
– *Joshua Retold: Synoptic Perspectives* (Edinburgh: T. & T. Clark, 1998).

Blenkinsopp, J. *The Pentateuch: An Introduction to the First Five Books of the Bible* (London: SCM, 1992; New York: Doubleday, 2000).

Dozeman, Thomas, Thomas Römer and Konrad Schmid (eds.), *Pentateuch, Hexateuch, or Enneateuch? Identifying Literary Works in Genesis through Kings* (Ancient Israel and its Literature, 8; Atlanta, GA: Society of Biblical Literature, 2011).

Dozeman, Thomas, and Konrad Schmid (eds.). *Farewell to the Yahwist* (SBLSymS, 34; Atlanta, GA: Society of Biblical Literature, 2006).

Driver, S.R. *An Introduction to the Literature of the Old Testament* (Edinburgh: T. & T. Clark, third edn, 1892).

Freedman, D.N. 'Hexateuch'; *IDB* vol. 2, 1962, pp. 597-98.

Goldingay, John E. *Models for Scripture* (Grand Rapids, MI: Eerdmans/Carlisle: Paternoster, 1994).

Nelson, Richard D. 'Josiah in the Book of Joshua', *JBL* 100 (1981), pp. 531-40.

Noth, M. *Überlieferungsgeschichtliche Studien* (Tübingen: Max Niemeyer, third edition 1957, original 1943), pp. 1-110, translated as *The Deuteronomistic History* (Sheffield: JSOT Press, 1981).

Rad, Gerhard von. 'The Form-Critical Problem of the Hexateuch', in his *The Problem of the Hexateuch and Other Essays* (London: Oliver & Boyd, 1966; London: SCM Press, 1984), pp. 1-78.

Schmid, Konrad. *Erzväter und Exodus: Untersuchungen zur doppelten Begründung der Ursprünge Israels innerhalb der Geschichtsbücher des Alten Testaments* (WMANT, 81; Neukirchen–Vluyn: Neukirchener Verlag, 1999).

– 'The Emergence and the Disappearance of the Separation between the Pentateuch and the Deuteronomistic History in Biblical Studies', in Dozeman *et al.* (2011), pp. 11-24.

Smend, R. 'Das Gesetz und die Völker: Ein Beitrag zur deuteronomistischen Redaktionsgeschichte', in H.-W. Wolff (ed.), *Probleme biblischer Theologie: Gerhard von Rad zum 70. Geburtstag* (Munich: Kaiser, 1971), translated as 'The Law and the Nations: A Contribution to Deuteronomistic Tradition History', in G.N. Knoppers and J.G. McConville (eds.). *Reconsidering Israel and Judah: Recent Studies on the Deuteronomistic History* (SBTS, 8; Winona Lake, IN: Eisenbrauns, 2000), pp. 95-110.

Vos, Jacobus Cornelis de. *Das Los Judas: Über Entstehung und Ziele der Landbeschreibung in Josua 15* (VTSup, 95; Leiden: Brill, 2003).

Younger, K. Lawson. *Ancient Conquest Accounts: A Study in Ancient Near Eastern and Biblical History Writing* (JSOTSup, 98; Sheffield: Sheffield Academic Press, 1990).

Joshua as Literature

In the preceding chapter, we considered the literary criticism of Joshua in the sense of the analysis of the formation of the book over time. We turn now to think about a different kind of literary approach, in which Joshua is treated as a work of literature. This approach, which may be dated roughly to the 1970s and which is now a vigorous branch of Old Testament study, is less interested in redactions of the book or in what can be known about the circumstances and theological rivalries that may have given rise to these. Rather, it concentrates on the literary features as such, namely plot, structure, narrative style, scene-changes and characterization (see Bar-Efrat 1989). Broadly speaking, therefore, it directs its attention to the text as a given thing, regardless of the process that produced it. Another way of saying this is that it focuses on the 'final form' of the text. That is less satisfactory, however, since the notion of 'final form' is misleading. Arguably, we do not have 'final forms' of biblical books, but only different extant versions, including, for the Old Testament, MT and LXX. Books of the Old Testament existed in different forms, as we know not only from LXX, but also from the scrolls discovered at Qumran, which counted among them, in some cases, different textual forms of the same book.

It follows that the formation of Old Testament books has no definitive end-point and the kind of study we observed in the preceding chapter might, in principle, be prolonged indefinitely in an attempt to describe exhaustively the process of a book's formation. In effect, literary approaches apply, not to the 'final form' of a text, but to a selected extant text, typically the MT. For completeness, it should be said that both MT and LXX represent 'canonical' forms of the text, and therefore aim to fix the development of a book, at a certain point, as canonical Scripture. However, canonical decisions are also selective and, as we have seen, the two canonical versions of Joshua diverge in important respects, not least on the ending of the book.

This approach to an extant text as literature may be regarded as a complementary method to the more historically orientated one that looks for original units and series of redactions. They are not ultimately separable, however, since literary approaches often operate on certain broad assumptions about the milieu of a text's production and can be interested in the audiences for which it might have been written. This is true especially of what is called 'rhetorical criticism', which is concerned with the capacity of a text to persuade an audience and regards this as one of its inherent features (Patrick and Scult 1990).

Yet one aspect of the emergence of literary approaches was an impatience with traditional criticism's relentless search for 'original' units and its extremely detailed accounts of a text's formation. A classic expression of this was Clines' critique of 'atomism' and 'geneticism' in his work on the Pentateuch, which traced a single theme throughout it, without regard for putative sources underlying it (Clines 1997). Others have been critical of the kind of methodology examined in the preceding chapter on the grounds that, by means of its redactional theories, it imposes reductive meanings on texts based on the supposed purposes of hypothetical redactors when the texts might actually be far more subtle than the theories allow (Provan 1997: 94).

Reading Joshua as a Book

Meaning in Narrative

As a starting-point for a literary approach to Joshua, it is worth returning to one of the features that played an important role in the redactional criticism of the book, namely the tension that exists between statements that report a total conquest (such as Josh. 11.23) and those that claim there remains much to do to overcome enemies and possess the land (e.g. Josh. 13.1). Instead of seeing such tensions as redactional clues, a literary approach asks whether the juxtaposition of tensions and contradictions of this sort contributes to the meaning of the book. Could it be that the reader is invited to query the surface meaning of a text like 11.23 simply because it is followed so soon by 13.1?

The modern classic example of such an approach is Robert Polzin. In his *Moses and the Deuteronomist*, he deals with Deuteronomy, Joshua and Judges and declares at the outset what he sees as the failure of historical-critical study (that is, source- and redaction-criticism) to produce satisfactory interpretations of the text (Polzin 1980: 12-16). He takes the 'Deuteronomic History' from the outset as a unified work and calls its author 'the Deuteronomist'. However, what he means by this is very different from what was meant by Martin Noth and the other authors discussed in the preceding chapter, with whom he enters into virtually no dialogue. His 'Deuteronomist' is simply the conventional name for the author of Deuteronomy–Kings, but he begins with no assumptions about that author's point of view or ideology.

Instead, he proposes to learn the meaning of the text from a close study of the text itself. It might be observed that in selecting Deuteronomy–Kings as a given text, he is actually adopting the redactional-critical postulate of Martin Noth. When he wrote, in 1980, that hypothesis seemed more secure than it does now. At least as good a case could be made for basing an analysis of the sort he proposes on Genesis–Kings as a whole.

Polzin's thesis is based on developments in the study of a broader range of literature than just that of the Bible. For him, the 'Deuteronomist' is identical with the 'implied author' (Polzin 1980: 18). The notion of an 'implied author' is a powerful hermeneutical device. It does not depend on knowing who the actual author was, and in fact is distinguished in principle from that author. Rather, the implied (or model) author is the author of a text as imagined and constructed by the reader as the reader engages with the text (Eco 1992: 64). He or she is the author required for the reader (or strictly the 'implied reader') to make sense of the text. The effect of this is to locate meaning in the activity of interpretation, rather than in the supposed programme of an empirical author or group, such as, in this case, 'the Deuteronomists'. It follows that the image of the implied author is not static, but open to change as the reading process develops. It should also be said that it is contingent on the body of literature selected as a 'work' (and therefore the implied author of Joshua is not necessarily identical with that of the 'Deuteronomistic History', though Polzin does not make this distinction in his treatment of Joshua).

Polzin therefore seeks the meaning of the book of Joshua not in head-line texts, nor in the words of Joshua, nor even the words of God, but rather in the position articulated by the dominant voice of the narrative or, in Mikhail Bakhtin's terms, the 'ultimate semantic authority' of the text (functionally equivalent to the 'implied author'; Polzin 1980: 21; cf. Eslinger 1989: 53-54). From this point of view, the reader must be aware that any individual statement, speech or point of view in the book, rather than being simply advocated, may be held up to critical scrutiny by the narrative voice (pp. 73-74). The intention of that voice has to be read out of the narrative as a whole, with the interrelationship of all its parts playing into it.

In this approach to Joshua, it is precisely in its discrepancies that the meaning of the book of Joshua is to be sought. The most salient of these is the clashing perspectives on the fulfilment of the promise of complete conquest. According to Polzin, we have, in chaps. 2–12, 'a polemic response to a simplistic characterization of Joshua's and Israel's fulfillment of God's commands (Polzin p. 80). The discrepancy between the two perspectives continues through the book and may be analyzed in depth. Eslinger points to evaluations of the success of the conquest variously in the mouths of

Joshua, Yahweh and the narrator. Joshua claims a complete conquest in 22.4, but he then undermines it by what he says in 23.4-5, where not only is the incompleteness of the conquest implied, but also the shocking idea that, not the land, but the remaining nations themselves are Israel's 'inheritance' (Eslinger 1984: 30-31). Yahweh's only direct evaluation affirms the incompleteness of the conquest and thus pits God's word against the narrator's overt position (pp. 29-30). The narrator's own positive evaluations stand in conflict with the story that he or she actually unfolds (p. 31).

Total Conquest? Rahab and the Gibeonites

The story of Rahab is a test-case for both Polzin and Eslinger. Following Joshua 1, with its affirmation that Yahweh has already given the land to Israel and the presentation of Joshua as ready to keep the Torah and act courageously according to Yahweh's command, it is surprising to find Joshua sending spies. Is Joshua as strong as he is made out to be? And does not the whole mission smack of compromise, since the spies' promise to Rahab precisely contravenes the rules for war in the promised land in Deut. 20.15-18 (Polzin 1980: 86). The episode is also reminiscent of the role of spies in a previous failure to enter the land (in Numbers 13–14; Eslinger 1984: 35). We have already noticed some of the oddities of the story, not least that a Canaanite prostitute should apparently play a role in the success of the Israelite mission. It is odd that Rahab should be so well-versed in Israelite theology, convinced not only that Israel would overcome her people and possess their land, but that this was by the gift of Yahweh, who had also caused them to 'melt in fear' before them and this in express connection with the exodus from Egypt and the victories over Sihon and Og in Transjordan (Josh. 2.11; cf. Deut. 2.24-25). For Eslinger, the sheer unlikelihood of this is a signal by the narrator that it should not be taken at face value (Eslinger 1984: 37-38). The story as a whole actually makes clear that the spies' mission was not at all necessary, partly because the action in chap. 2 achieves nothing significant for the spies or Israel and partly because, in the end, Jericho would fall by miraculous means, regardless of anything the spies might have gleaned.

The story of Rahab gives the impression that the narrator is deliberately undermining the surface statements of the narrative itself.

The Rahab episode may be compared with that of the Gibeonites (chap. 9), in which the citizens of Gibeon trick Joshua into allowing them to remain in the land alongside the Israelites. Here is another exception to the blanket command to carry out the *ḥērem* against the whole population. Eslinger estimates that these two stories together form 47% of chaps. 1–12 and sees this as a massive indication that the postulate of complete success in implementing the terms of the covenant is negated by the narrative (Eslinger 1984: 52).

The disharmonies in chaps. 2–12 do not stop there. It is curious that the total *ḥērem* demanded for Jericho was relaxed by Yahweh for Ai (Josh 8.2). And it is also extraordinary that the leniency towards Rahab and the Gibeonites with respect to the terms of the *ḥērem* contrasts so starkly with their stringent application in the case of the Israelite Achan and his family (chap. 7) because of their breach of those terms.

It will be clear that the kind of reading advocated by this approach sits uncomfortably with the redactional one. The idea of a Hexateuch redactor, for example, was predicated on the belief that there must have been a narrative of the occupation of the promised land to correspond to the Pentateuchal promises. But advocates of the literary approach cast doubt on whether the book of Joshua fulfils the criteria for a story of fulfilment. The kind of inner dialogue proposed in this approach does not resolve easily into the redactorial debates that we observed in the preceding chapter.

The basic issues raised here play out in further ways to which we now turn.

Israel's Land: The Jordan as Boundary?

The storyline of Joshua, on the surface, is that a nation called Israel, who had come out of Egypt, makes a decisive 'crossing' into a land that they come to possess by conquest and where they continue as an identifiable nation, separate from all others. However, when we look more closely, we find that here, too, the narrative gives signals, by various formal means, that cause us to question this premise. Not only does the book challenge its own overt assertions about total conquest, but it also raises doubts about whether Israel made a decisive 'crossing' or had a clear identity as a homogeneous people. In a book that devotes much space to boundaries and distinctiveness, do we know what Israel's borders really are, or who indeed constitutes the people of Israel?

The 'crossing' theme, as we saw in Chapter 1, was strongly emphasized in Joshua 3–4, where the verb *'ābar*, 'cross', occurs 21 times in connection with passing through the Jordan. The frequent repetition is a literary signal suggesting that the event has meaning beyond the physical crossing of a river and indicating a profound transition from one kind of life to another. This point is strengthened by the explicit analogy between the crossing of Jordan and the earlier crossing of the Reed Sea (4.23), that symbolic deliverance from slavery into freedom. The theme of separation is developed in Chapter 5, with its renewed distinction between the generation of the conquest and that which had died in the wilderness because of lack of faith, together with its separation rituals of circumcision and Passover. The significance of the Jordan as a boundary is heightened by the appearance of the 'commander of Yahweh's armies', with its echo of Moses' encounter with Yahweh at Horeb (Exod. 3.1-6), and the designation of this border-place as 'holy' (5.15). The 'crossing' motif then continues in the account of Jericho, with its striking three-fold repetition of *'ābar* in 6.7-8. Translations normally obscure this, adopting terms such as 'go forward' and 'pass on', because the particular actions described are not readily imaginable as 'crossing' anything. The usage, therefore, is a literary device, creatively unifying the crossing of the Jordan and the conquest of Jericho, to convey the point that the entire process of entering the land and defeating its occupants to possess it counts as a 'crossing' into a new kind of life. The language guides the reader to see that the physical actions described have deeper, symbolic meaning.

The symbolism in the Jericho narrative is evident in other ways. The siege of the city is given a specifically religious accent by the usage of the numbers six and seven, in the stylized account of the repeated processions around the city. The six days plus one (6.3-4) evoke the week of creation culminating in the Sabbath (Genesis 1). The phrase 'seven trumpets of rams' horns' (*šib'â šôprôt hayyôbᵉlîm*) oddly combines the two words *šôpār* and *yôbēl*. The word *yôbēl* means both 'ram's horn' and 'Jubilee' and so, by a play on words, the effect of this phrase, in Josh. 6.4, is to recall the celebration of the Jubilee, which is announced by the sounding of the trumpet (*šôpār*) and then the Jubilee itself (*yôbēl*) is proclaimed (Lev. 25.9-10). The word *yôbēl* occurs almost exclusively in Leviticus 25 and 27 and Joshua 6 (exceptions are Exod. 19.13 and Num. 36.4). It follows that Joshua 6 is a careful literary composition designed to interpret the conquest of Jericho theologically as an act of creation, by virtue of its echoes of Genesis 1, of separation (by its use of *'ābar*, 'cross') and of liberation, through its evocation of the Jubilee.

The narrative of Joshua 3–6, therefore, is framed to articulate the theology of 'crossing', by which Israel is established in its promised land as a distinctive nation. Yet this theme, like that of 'total conquest', is also undermined in the discourse of the book. Given the prominence of the crossing of the Jordan as a premise for the success of Israel, it is surprising that the Jordan's status as a boundary comes into question repeatedly. This is a function of the portrayal of the two and a half Transjordanian tribes in relation to the nine and a half in the west. Again, there are literary aspects to this topic that serve to articulate a viewpoint. The exceptional status of the Transjordanians is indicated not least by their repeated occurrence at prominent places in the book. As in Deuteronomy (Deut. 2.16–3.22), so in Joshua, the special treatment of Reuben, Gad and half-Manasseh is described at the outset (Josh. 1.12-18) by way of a prelude to the main action. Indeed, in Joshua 1, it is a kind of interruption, following awkwardly on the command to prepare for the crossing of the Jordan in 1.11 (and so leading into that further interruption in the narrative of Rahab, chap. 2). Then the topic recurs on the threshold of the distribution of the land (13.7-33), now providing for the distribution of territory in Transjordan and, once again, as a kind of interruption following a command to take 'the land that remains', that is, west of the river (13.1-7).

The effect of the account in 13.7-33 is precisely to focus on the status of the river Jordan as a boundary. This emerges tellingly in 13.23, with its awkward repetition of the word *gᵉbûl* ('boundary'). We noticed above (Chapter 1), that this term served to emphasize the importance of territorial demarcations in the distribution of land, even being imposed on the material in unexpected ways. Josh. 13.23 fits with this, but so as to direct attention to the debatable status of the Jordan as a boundary.

The topic re-appears in 14.3-4, where its effect begins to become clear, namely that the great project of crossing the Jordan was actually for the benefit not of Israel as a whole, but of nine and a half tribes only. (The number twelve is made up by Levi, which was not to have a regional inheritance). The repetition of the position of the Transjordanians seems intended to keep the non-integrity of Israel as a nation that has crossed the Jordan in the forefront of the unfolding picture.

This thread in the narrative reaches its climax in chap. 22, where the division between east and west of the Jordan is exposed in open confrontation (see above, Chapter 1: Outline). The topic thus asserts itself near the end of the book, as it had done at the beginning. As a function of the form of the book, this gives it considerable prominence and places it in counterpoint with the symbolism of the Jordan in chaps. 3–6. The conflict, occasioned by the setting up of the altar at the Jordan, testifies to a doubt in the minds of the 'westerners' about the commitment of the Transjordanians to be fully part of Israel. The ambiguity of the structure itself symbolizes this doubt. The Transjordanians assert their intention to remain fully integrated (22.24-28). But, as so often, we have to interpret the words of the characters in relation to the dominant tendency of the text. And there is a counterpoint to the 'easterners'' self-presentation in the ways in which their territory is described. Its designation as 'the land of Gilead' is in express opposition to 'the land of Canaan' (Josh. 22.9, 32; cf. Num. 32.29, 32), where the latter phrase denotes the territory west of the Jordan. Significantly, the latter is also called 'Yahweh's land', as opposed to 'your land', with the added hint that it may be 'unclean' (22.19). Even the form 'the land where the Reubenites and Gadites were dwelling' (22.33), is consistent with its portrayal as different from the 'real' land of Israel. These are signals that the Jordan as a boundary has a debatable status. It is not saying outright that the Transjordanians are not part of Israel proper. Rather, as Jobling has argued, the text indicates an ambiguity in their status. 'It [Transjordan] belongs at some level to Israel; yet there is a suspicion of another level at which it belongs rather to someone else, so that Israel's occupation of it is not Yahweh's intention...' (Jobling 1986: 116-17). The significance for theology is that Israel may not finally be determined by the precise definition of its land (cf. Earl 2010: 92). (This has implications for the way in which Joshua is sometimes used in relation to land-possession today. See below, Chapter 6.)

Israel as a Separated People?

The storyline of Joshua is focused on a people and a land. We have seen that the exact boundaries of the land have been put in question. We shall now see that the same also applies to the people. We have so far considered the Rahab story as a clue to the way in which literary features of Joshua alert the reader to question the surface tendencies of the text. It was surprising that a Canaanite prostitute should have a role in facilitating the conquest when this has first been presented as something that Yahweh has already determined upon. The same narrative also introduces the topic of the nature of Israel. Joshua's indulgence towards Rahab and her family (Josh. 6.22-25) is in direct opposition to the terms of the *ḥērem* (vv. 17-19). This has a disturbing effect on the composition of Israel. The *ḥērem* was intended to mark the clean separation between Israel and the peoples of the land, but this is precisely what is compromised by the exception made for Rahab. For not only are Rahab and her family spared in the destruction of Jericho, but they also continue alongside Israel in the land. Their status is somewhat ambiguous: on one hand, when they are brought out of the city, they are set 'outside the camp' of Israel (6.23); on the other, they are said to dwell 'in the midst of Israel to this day' (6.25).

How are we as readers to evaluate this? The exception made for Rahab is supplied with an apparent justification, namely that she protected Joshua's spies (6.25). But, as readers, are we expected to accept this as a sufficient or acceptable explanation? We have already commented on the dubious status of the spies' mission itself. We have seen too that the words and actions of the characters in the narrative are not to be equated with the overarching viewpoint of the book and it is noteworthy here that the sparing of Rahab, with its prelude in the mission of the spies, is only ever at the behest of Joshua, not of Yahweh (6.17, 22; cf. 2.1).

The Rahab episode has to be taken together with that of the Gibeonites (chap. 9), who trick Joshua and Israel's leaders by appearing to be travellers from another country (9.6). The point of their deception is explained by the terms of the *ḥērem*, which made a distinction between people who lived in the land and those from outside (Deut. 20.10-18), only the former being subject to the *ḥērem*. As a result, the inhabitants of Gibeon and its surrounding towns are spared the *ḥērem*, and, like Rahab, continue to live alongside the Israelites 'to this day', albeit in a servant capacity (9.27). The episode betrays once again the frailty of the characters' understanding and the ambiguity in the narrative. When they discover the Gibeonites' trickery, the Israelite leaders decide they cannot harm them because they (Israel) have sworn an oath by Yahweh not to do so (9.19). Once again, the reader is perplexed. Does this oath in Yahweh's name now take precedence over Yahweh's own command to carry out the *ḥērem* and should we trust the leaders' judgment on it? Their failure to perceive the Gibeonites' trickery in the first place is expressly noted in the narrator's comment that they did not seek guidance from God when they decided to believe the Gibeonites' story (9.14).

Situated between the stories of Rahab-Jericho and Gibeon comes the quite different account of the Israelite Achan, who with his family is subjected to the *ḥērem* for keeping some of the proscribed plunder from Jericho for himself (7.1). Paradoxically, while certain Canaanites are exempted from the terms of the *ḥērem* and permitted to live among the Israelites, this Israelite is treated strictly according to its terms and excised from Israel in the most radical way. As Hawk has shown, the sequence of stories reflects on the topic of 'insiders' and 'outsiders', in which unexpected reversals take place. In chap. 2, for example, Rahab, the outsider, utters a confession of praise to Yahweh while the Israelite spies do not (Hawk 2000: 46; cf. Hawk 1991). Who are the real 'insiders' (native-born Israelites?) and 'outsiders' (Canaanites?)? The corollary of the whole nexus from Rahab to Gibeon, including Achan, is that 'Israel' cannot simply be equated with the people who crossed the Jordan: there are those 'within' who may be outsiders, and those 'without' who may become, in effect, part of Israel. At stake is the question of Israelite identity. In a world in which, in practice, people of many beliefs and allegiances lived alongside each other, who truly constituted Israel? (See also Earl 2010: 64-99.) As with the extent of the land, so with the people themselves, questions of definition are to the fore. The ostensible storyline – that Israel, as a unified people, is distinguished from the peoples of the land by conquest and *ḥērem* – is once again undermined by the text, as read with attention to its literary form (Eslinger 1984: 33, on Rahab, following Polzin).

Conclusion

In the present chapter, we have drawn attention to the relationship between the form of the text and its meaning. Features which in redaction criticism are taken as evidence of a work's redactional history and as reflecting disparate points of view embedded in an evolving text, are seen here as part of what constitutes the text's meaning. Superficially perplexing connections, such as the discrepancy between claims about complete and incomplete conquest, may be of the essence. Surface statements of any character need to be scrutinized critically in terms of the text's overall direction. This must enter into an evaluation even of the divine command to kill all the Canaanites. How does this sit in the end with the apparent acceptance that Israel's life in the land – 'to this day' – actually plays out alongside others? When we look beneath the surface of the text, some of its biggest questions are put in a new light. In the case of the *ḥērem* itself, that crucial concept in Joshua, it is important to look afresh at what it is intended to convey. For Earl, it symbolizes response to God's action in the world, 'serving the function of a text that indicates where one's heart and true identity are located' (Earl 2010: 96).

The point holds true for many features of the book, such as Joshua's extraordinary declaration near its conclusion, in the context of the covenant-renewal at Shechem: 'You cannot serve the LORD…he will not forgive your transgressions or your sins' (24.19 NRSV). When we realize that the speakers in the narrative are fallible in their judgments and do not necessarily articulate the intention of the text (in Eco's terms), we do not have to take this as a straightforward theological truth. Rather, it has its meaning in relation to the whole. The twin idea that Israel cannot keep the very covenant it is in the act of entering into and that God will not forgive their sins draws attention to a paradoxical feature of Deuteronomic theology, expressed in its account of the Golden Calf apostasy (Deuteronomy 9–10), and especially in Deut. 9.4-6. Here too, Israel's incapacity to keep the covenant is asserted in the context of Deuteronomy's extended exhortations to do precisely that. The paradox is used rhetorically to stress the absolutely prior role of God's gift and grace in Israel's life. As Polzin has seen, the function of Joshua's discourse and rhetoric is indebted to this theology; by putting Israel and the Canaanites (like Rahab) on an equal footing, God's grace in relation to Israel's life is underscored: '…*the story of Rahab is really the story of Israel*…' (Polzin 1980: 88, emphasis original); and 'Rahab is allowed to settle permanently in the midst of Israel for exactly the same reasons that Israel is allowed to settle permanently in her homeland' (Polzin 1980, 89). The point depends, of course, partly on confirming Joshua's words, at least in a certain sense ('You cannot serve the LORD'), and partly on negating them: 'he will not forgive your transgressions or your sins'. The possibility of forgiveness is not actually foreclosed by this; indeed, it is apparently the only basis on which the covenant can be maintained. This point emerges, however, from reading the text as a whole with a close eye on the signals it gives about its meaning, which, as we have seen, often does not lie on the surface. The point of this is not to set puzzles, but to invite critical reflection on the very kinds of theological affirmations that do lie on the surface.

Bibliography

Bar-Efrat, S. *Narrative Art in the Bible* (JSOTSup, 70; Sheffield: Almond Press, 1989).

Clines, D.J.A. *The Theme of the Pentateuch* (Sheffield: Sheffield Academic Press, second edn, 1997 [first edn, 1978]).

Earl, Douglas S. *The Joshua Delusion: Rethinking Genocide in the Bible* (Eugene, OR: Cascade Books, 2010).

Eco, Umberto. 'Overinterpreting Texts', in Stefan Collini (ed.), *Interpretation and Overinterpretation* (Cambridge: Cambridge University Press, 1992), pp. 45-66.

Eslinger, Lyle. *Into the Hands of the Living God* (JSOTSup, 84; Sheffield: Almond Press, 1984).

Hawk, L. Daniel., *Joshua* (Berit Olam; Collegeville, MI: Liturgical Press, 2000).

—*Every Promise Fulfilled: Contesting Plots in Joshua* (LCBI; Louisville, KY: Westminster John Knox Press, 1991).

Jobling, David. '"The Jordan a Boundary": Transjordan in Israel's Ideological Geography', in *The Sense of Biblical Narrative II* (JSOTSup, 39; Sheffield: JSOT Press, 1986), pp. 88-123.

Patrick, Dale and Allen Scult. *Rhetoric and Biblical Interpretation* (Sheffield: Almond Press, 1990).

Polzin, Robert. *Moses and the Deuteronomist* (New York: Seabury Press, 1980).

Provan, I. *1 and 2 Kings* (OTG; Sheffield: Sheffield Academic Press, 1997).

Joshua and Genre: History and Myth

It is obvious that the book of Joshua deals in some way with history. It is less obvious in what sense that is so. In the following pages we will consider the book in relation to the historical question of the beginnings of Israel and ask in what sense it may be regarded as historiography. That is, what sort of book is Joshua and what does it purport to do in relation to Israel's consciousness of its origins and destiny?

These questions follow from what we have seen in the preceding chapters. It has become clear from a close literary reading of the book that it does not recount historical events in a straightforward manner. On the basis of the most striking discrepancy that we have observed, the historian is bound to ask: did Joshua subjugate the land completely, or not? As a matter of historical record, these perspectives cannot both be true. There are, no doubt, good reasons why the book organizes its narrative in the way it does and we have begun to explore these in the preceding chapters (and will do so again below). But with regard to historical reporting, the book's own communicative strategy invites us to be cautious and critical. Many of the features we observed feed into such an enquiry. For example, does the evident concentration on certain tribes, especially the tribe of Judah, and the uneven distribution of what might be seen as historical detail (in the conquest reports and in the accounts of settlement) suggest that the historical perspective is not that of the earliest appearance of Israel in the land, but rather that of a later time, when issues facing the people were quite different? If so, the book of Joshua would not simply be a record of how Israel came to be in its land, but an appraisal of Israel's place and identity in which a narrative of origins serves as an analogy, or a mirror, for the purpose of self-knowledge, critique, and perhaps encouragement.

It can quite properly be replied to this that there is no such thing as entirely objective history-telling. There are no 'brute facts'; rather, all history is narrative and interpretation, inevitably from a certain point of view. And this must be conceded in principle. Joshua, therefore, might be regarded as an account of history in which the point of view happens to be theological, namely that Yahweh, the God of Israel, is powerful and sovereign in all of human affairs and events. Many contemporary works on Joshua take precisely this view (e.g. Hess 1996: 17-62).

However, the questions asked above remain. Any rendering of past events, if it is to count as historical, must be capable of being interrogated for factual accuracy. Biblical books are no exception to this. Indeed, we owe it to them, in order to be clear what it is that they aim to say to us. Finally, it should be said that our question is not even simply a matter of establishing whether or not events reported in Joshua actually happened. The question regarding the genre and purpose of Joshua will still remain.

A Historical Conquest?

The historical picture given by the book of Joshua is of a conquest of Canaan by an invading people of Israel, fully formed as twelve tribes, having recently escaped from an existence as slaves in Egypt. This picture was broadly followed, at least in outline, by a significant segment of scholarship in the mid- to late twentieth century, and Israel's arrival in Canaan was generally ascribed to the late thirteenth century BCE. The biblical picture assumed a lapse of time between Joshua and King David, which is taken up by the 'Judges period' (as in the book of Judges) and the events leading up to the establishment of the monarchy (1 Samuel 1–12). Those events testify to some contention over that form of rule, suggesting that early Israel was characterized by a certain view of political authority, which was suspicious of kingship. The Old Testament provides a chronology placing the conquest 480 years before Solomon laid the foundation of the temple (1 Kgs 6.1). As the latter event is dated around 966 BCE, the conquest would have taken place in the mid-fifteenth century. The three hundred years in Judg. 11.26 would also contribute to a dating of this sort. A fifteenth-century date for the origin of Israel has been maintained on the basis of a reading of the archaeological record and relative ancient Near Eastern chronology (Bimson 1981, 1989) and has had a certain following (see Howard 1998: 31, notes 10, 12). However, the conquest was generally not put as early as that, for two reasons. Firstly, the chronological data in Judges–Samuel are not self-consistent; when all the periods of time specified in those books are added together they are rather longer than the 480 years of 1 Kgs 6.1. This figure, therefore, has been taken as a round figure, or symbolic number, perhaps twelve times forty, denoting respectively the number of the tribes and the notional length of a generation (Howard 1998: 32-33).

Secondly, the thirteenth century is favoured by extra-biblical evidence. One independent witness is provided by the victory stele of Pharaoh Merneptah (the Merneptah Stele, 1230 BCE). At this time, Egypt was the dominant power in Canaan, and the stele commemorates this Pharaoh's victorious campaign against certain population elements in the area, one of which was a people called 'Israel'. This is therefore the first historical reference to Israel outside the Bible. The stele gives no further information about the extent or development of Israel at the time or what exactly is meant by 'a people'. However, that period also appears, from the archaeological record, to have seen a significant decline in Canaanite city-culture. These two factors suggested the second half of the thirteenth century as a likely time for the arrival of a vigorous new people in the land.

The biblical picture constituted the frame for a view of the history of Israel that was maintained in significant strands of scholarship in the middle of the twentieth century. In the work of W.F. Albright, John Bright and Kenneth Kitchen among others, the portrayal of Israel's history lay close to the biblical picture. This approach continues to find advocates today among commentators on Joshua (e.g. Hess, Howard, Pitkänen). There were also variations of it, in which the idea of conquest was replaced by theories of 'infiltration' (M. Noth), or some kind of political revolt (N. Gottwald), yet these remained broadly influenced by the biblical picture.

However, this position has been strongly challenged in recent times. As Rösel puts it, 'the concept of a military conquest by a united people called Israel has been virtually abandoned by modern scholarship' (Rösel 2011: 97). The most common current view of Israel's origins is that it originated in a particular form of village settlement found in the central hill-country. The archaeological period of these unwalled villages is the late thirteenth and twelfth centuries BCE. Because their dwellers essentially shared the material culture of the Canaanite peoples of the land around them, there is no need to suppose that they came from outside the land. They are differentiated from the inhabitants of the cities in the lowlands and plain by the simplicity of their buildings and apparent absence of a sophisticated social or political structure (Nelson 1997: 3-5; cf. Fritz 1994: 9-14).

Archaeology and Sites in Joshua

Because Joshua tells of the occupation of the land of Canaan by Israel, its interpretation has generally made reference to archaeological investigations of sites that appear in the narrative. Some of these can be identified with more certainty than others. Jericho, for example, is universally identified as Tell es-Sultan, 16 km to the north of the Dead Sea, whereas there is no definite site for Gilgal. Archaeology can sometimes make a narrative look more probable, sometimes less so. Taken with other factors, it can help towards an understanding of how a narrative purporting to tell about historical events should be read.

Jericho supplies the most celebrated example of this relationship between narrative and archaeology in Joshua. Archaeological research finds no evidence of a walled city in the Late Bronze Age (LB) (Bienkowski 1986: 124-25, following the work of Kathleen Kenyon in the 1950s; cf. Rösel 2011: 97; Nelson 1997: 3). There was a flourishing city earlier, in the Middle Bronze Age (MB), but at most a limited settlement on the tell in the late thirteenth century, not a walled city. Bienkowski dates the latest significant settlement around 1275 BCE, somewhat too early for Joshua (Bienkowski 1986: 156).

It should be observed that the archaeological record at Jericho is somewhat confusing. One possibility is that walls from the Early Bronze (EB) and MB were simply used again by occupants in LB (Mazar 1992: 283; Kenyon 1957: 262). LB cities in Canaan were often small and did not always have their own fortifications (Bienkowski 1986: 124-25; Hess, 1996: 137-38). The site has also been subject to considerable erosion, due to long periods when it was not occupied, which means that the archaeologist contemplates a picture that is far from complete, and therefore hard to interpret. For example, it is possible that debris heaped against one of the MB walls could have fallen from a later wall at the top of the tell, now entirely eroded away (Kenyon 1957: 262; cf. Pitkänen 2010: 162-69). Mazar cautions against the confident assertion that the archaeology is simply incompatible with the biblical picture: 'in this case archaeological evidence does not run directly counter to the biblical tale, as is asserted by some scholars' (Mazar 1992: 283; for a similar view, see Kenyon in *NEAEHL* 2: 680).

However, other sites in the Joshua narrative throw up their own questions for the interpreter. Ai, widely identified as Et-Tell, was by all accounts not occupied in LB, though it began to be re-settled as a 'village' (i.e. unfortified) in the early Iron Age (*NEAEHL* 1: 44). This has led some to suggest alternative locations for Ai and, consequently, Bethel, or to suppose that Ai actually represents Bethel in the narrative, perhaps because its name (meaning 'ruin', or 'heap of stones') had a resonance that appealed to the author (see Hess 1996: 157-59). In this case, Mazar thinks that only an aetiological explanation is possible (Mazar 1992: 283 – that is, the story was told to explain the existence of the well-known heap of stones near Bethel). On Mt Ebal, cultic structures have been found which, according to the excavator A. Zertal, could include the altar built by Joshua for the ceremony in Josh. 8.30-35 (cited by Mazar, 1992: 293; cf. Hess, 1996: 174). But the identification of the rectangular structure in the middle of the site as an altar is uncertain. (Mazar is inclined to think it is the base of a tower; Mazar, 1992: 293-95 and illustration, p. 294). In any case, this site illustrates some basic problems in correlating archaeology with texts. If the site is indeed cultic, how would we decide whether this confirms the Joshua story, or whether, alternatively, the story is an aetiology based on the existence of the site? The archaeology does not preclude an assessment of the nature of the text on a variety of grounds, including literary and theological. Some recent appraisals regard Josh. 8.30-35 as thoroughly Deuteronomistic, and therefore as having no direct connection with an Iron Age sanctuary (Nelson 1997: 118 n. 5; Rösel 2011: 135-36; Na'aman 2000).

Border-Descriptions

Another kind of historical issue raised by the text of Joshua is the provenance of the concept of the extent of the land of Canaan found in the book and the descriptions of the internal borders between the tribal allotments.

For Kallai, the extent of the land of Canaan projected in a range of Old Testament texts reflects a basic pattern that exists in the minds of the biblical authors. In his view, 'the only background that could have served as a basis for such a description was the province of Canaan in the last period of Egyptian imperial rule' (Kallai 1998: 114; cf. pp. 112-13). Aharoni also thought the extent of the land of Canaan projected in Numbers and Joshua corresponds to Canaan as it was known under Egyptian administration in the fourteenth and thirteenth centuries BCE (Aharoni, 1961: 68). Aharoni concluded that the biblical description of the boundaries of Canaan accorded well with historical fact. Kallai, however, does not agree that the data support the factuality of the narrative of the conquest. Rather, he thinks the texts reflect various accommodations between the ancient concept and historical realities. One issue that illustrates this is the status of Transjordan, which, as we have noted several times already, is repeatedly highlighted in Joshua. In his view, Joshua is distinct from Numbers 32 and 34 in its presentation of Transjordan because it tends progressively to obscure the distinction between it and the western territory, a distinction that is clearly maintained in Numbers. Even so, one can still discern in Joshua traces of the old basic distinction between the two areas (Kallai 1998: 126-27). In this case then, as with the archaeology, attention to the historical data does not preclude careful analysis of the texts themselves. Kallai concludes his study of the topic in a range of Old Testament texts by proposing that it was the territorial extent of Israel in the kingdoms of David and Solomon, following the Davidic conquests, that 'served as the basis for the geographical concept found in these descriptions' (Kallai 1998: 128).

The internal tribal border-descriptions have also been variously dated. The lists concerning Judah in Josh. 15.21-63 have been mainly assigned to dates between the ninth and seventh centuries BCE. It is commonly thought that the lists are based on some kind of administrative arrangements, but it is hard to determine what these were or when they arose because there seems to be no single time that suits all the data (Rösel 2011: 245-46). We noted above (Chapter 2) the view of de Vos that many of the places named apparently did not exist in Joshua's purported lifetime, that is, the thirteenth century BCE. He thought that those that occur after Josh. 15.21 mostly came into being in the seventh century BCE (de Vos 2003: 6). Others have seen a development of the lists over time. Hess also notes, with reference to Judah's city-list, that it includes areas that were not settled until the monarchy period (Hess 1996: 246-47), but diverges from the usual view that the lists must be thought to reflect actual contemporary political conditions. His solution is that the texts and lists are, in principle separate from, and pre-date, the process of settlement and were used as reference-points for administrative purposes in that process (p. 249).

The case of the boundary-descriptions illustrates well the dilemmas involved in trying to relate the text of Joshua to the events that the book purports to describe. For most scholars, the relation of text to history is not a simple case of a once-for-all record of things that happened in Joshua's time, but rather the text was shaped over generations by evolving historical contingencies. There is admittedly much uncertainty in this. Indeed, uncertainty is in the nature of the kinds of enquiry that the data call for. It is clear that there will be no knock-down arguments one way or the other about historicity. Our brief survey of the issues shows, in contrast, that what is at stake is the nature of the text. In what way should we think that it relates to history? We turn now to consider this question.

A 'Conquest Account'?

We have been thinking about what kind of writing Joshua is. In a way, that is a question about 'genre'. But 'genre' can be a misleading term when it comes to asking whether a piece of writing might, in some sense, be 'history'. These days we may encounter 'history' in a number of genres. Television programmes, for example, can make quite serious claims to be doing history, yet are clearly not the same 'genre' as the textbooks traditionally used in school. There are even historical novels which make or imply some claim to be doing history and the boundary between 'historical novel' and 'novelized history' can be hard to discern. There is no separate 'genre' called 'history-writing'.

In ancient times, too, there were different genres that offered historical accounts. Van Seters shows that ancient Egyptian literature included a number of historical genres (Van Seters 1983: 128-87). Within the Old Testament, we see some signs of this in diverse reviews of Israel's history, as in the two accounts of Deborah and Barak's victory in Judges 4 and 5, in prophetic passages such as Amos 2.9-11 and in a liturgical piece such as Psalm 78. No doubt the senses in which these are 'historical' need to be carefully defined in each case, but the point is to counsel caution before deciding that any text either is or is not 'history' on the basis of expectations that are based on modern understandings, rather than ancient ones.

An important contribution to this question was made by K. Lawson Younger. He believes that, to understand Joshua, it is necessary to put it in the context of ancient Near Eastern conquest narratives (Younger 1990: 52). This involves paying attention to the way in which the text is constructed and written as a function of its meaning and recognizing that this is a distinct exercise from reconstructing the events that may have lain behind the text (p. 62). His point, therefore, is that it is misleading to distinguish in principle between 'history-writing' and 'literary production', because history-writing always takes literary form. That is, '…historians use the same techniques as literary artists to *arrange* or *fashion* their materials' (p. 41, emphasis original) and 'history writing is the imposing of an interpretive form on the past' (p. 44).

This means that the 'literary' features of Joshua do not necessarily prove that it is not, in some sense, history-writing. For Younger, the historian's message is 'encoded' (p. 45), that is, it is conveyed by means of a certain kind of language which can be recognized for what it is because it is familiar from a range of similar writings. And it includes literary devices such as hyperbole and synecdoche (examples below).

Just as ancient conquest accounts had literary characteristics, so too did they have 'ideological' features, that is, fundamental concepts about the nature of social reality. Common to ancient conquest accounts was a sense of an order in the world that was threatened by the presence or actions of enemies. In Egypt, for example, foreigners were typically portrayed as inferior and even evil. Conquest accounts, therefore, are conceived as overcoming chaos and re-establishing proper order (Younger, pp. 177-79, 194; cf. pp. 67-69 for Assyria).

For Younger, Joshua shares a basic 'transmission code' with ancient conquest accounts, consisting of an ideological and structural code, recurring themes and motifs and figurative language (pp. 70-71, 199). Episodes in an account have the same structural elements and there is frequent repetition of key language units (syntagms), with a strong tendency to 'redundance' (roughly, a linguistic overplus) in order to reinforce a message and communicate an ideology (pp. 71-72). (For a list of frequent syntagms in Assyrian accounts, see pp. 72-79.)

On the basis of an examination of Joshua 9–12 in the light of ancient Near Eastern parallels, Younger proposes a re-evaluation of the Joshua narrative. The Gibeonite episode, for example (Josh. 9), finds a parallel in an Egyptian conquest-account, in which the inhabitants of certain cities were terrified at the approach of the Egyptian king, submitted to him, and were integrated into his people (p. 200). Younger concludes that Joshua 9 'functions plausibly in its present context because it basically follows the same transmission code as observed in the ancient Near Eastern conquest accounts' (p. 204). This does not prove it is historical; but it shows at least that the author of Joshua 9 was aware of canons of history-writing that prevailed elsewhere in his world. By the same token, it is not necessary to attribute the story to a separate 'tradition' from the other material in chaps. 10–12.

Younger's analysis applies to other features that we have observed in Joshua. For instance, the picture of a 'total conquest', as in texts such as Joshua 11, should be understood to be figurative and hyperbolic (pp. 242-43, 251). In the transmission code, 'conquest' may not mean total subjugation (as apparently implied in the language of Josh. 9.1, for example; pp. 243-44). The repeated use of terms for totality is common and stereotypical. He cites an Egyptian text for the repeated and hyperbolic use of 'all' (p. 245). Thus, there is no real conflict between the perspective of a total conquest and those texts that show that the conquest was, in fact, gradual and incomplete. All such texts belong together in accounts that purport to tell 'history' (pp. 245-46). In particular, he argues against the notion of a 'total conquest' redaction (p. 247). Similarly, the idea of 'all Israel' is 'nothing more than a commonly encountered synecdoche' (e.g. Josh. 10.29; 248), and therefore, likewise, there is no need to postulate a 'pan-Israelite' redaction (p. 247). (Synecdoche is a figure of speech in which either the whole may stand for the part – as in this case – or the part for the whole.)

Finally, Joshua shares fundamental ideological features with these neighbouring nations, namely: 'a similar view of the enemy, calculated terror, the high use of hyperbole, a jural aspect [roughly: 'they deserved it'], and the use of stereotyped syntagms to transmit the high-redundance message of the ideology' (p. 253). The point serves to argue that theologized accounts of victories, even exaggerated ones such as Joshua 6, are exactly what one would expect in a world in which all events are attributed to a deity, who acts on behalf of his own special people (pp. 258-60).

Younger's thesis warns against dismissing too readily the idea that Joshua may properly be described as history-writing. It puts a distinctive light on some of the issues we have been concerned with. The discrepancy between the depictions of the conquest as complete and incomplete is here explained, not as the clever irony of a sophisticated writer (Polzin), but as deriving from well-known ancient habits of writing about conquests. Hyperbole is not the same as irony. It is possible that these two approaches may be reconciled. A clever writer might have found the basic pattern of a conquest account an ideal vehicle for an ironic story about Israel. However, in view of Younger's comparison of Joshua with ancient Near Eastern accounts, the literary observations we made in the preceding chapter should not be taken as evidence in themselves that the book implies no claim to tell history. (A similar point is made by Stephen Williams, in McConville and Williams 2010: 212.)

Nevertheless, the identification of Joshua as a 'conquest account' according to ancient Near eastern convention does not yield the conclusion that it is a factual account of events. Younger makes it clear that its conformity to certain conventional expectations is an indicator of its interest above all in conveying a certain meaning through the act of narrating events. Historical narrative is always 'figurative' (Younger, p. 45). It follows that the classification of Joshua as a 'conquest account' does not make other kinds of historical research redundant. These proceed according to their own canons and it remains an open question just how the book's account of Israel's arrival in the land relates to the picture built up by scholars in other ways.

Joshua as Myth?

Since Joshua is interested in interpreting the meaning of the formative events in Israel's existence in the land, the question is raised whether it might properly be regarded as 'myth'. Younger thought that 'myth' was applicable more properly to a stage of oral literacy and that oral cultures tended to adapt the past to present needs (Younger, p. 46). Yet he did think Joshua's history-writing was 'figurative' and it may be that the distinction between oral and written is not absolute in this respect. More recently, Douglas Earl has found the concept of myth useful for understanding how the narrative of Joshua might have helped its ancient audience to shape its self-understanding, or identity, as a people. The ways in which societies understand themselves are manifest, for example, in institutions or in symbolic actions. These can express beliefs, values, purpose and a sense of how the society in question takes its place in the wider world (Earl 2010: 16).

Certain narratives, too, may have the character of 'myth'. To read Joshua in this way would imply recognizing that its significance is not necessarily defined by a surface, or 'literal', meaning. It could, therefore, testify to 'an imaginative world that seeks to shape the way in which the community and the individual lives, thinks and feels...' (Earl 2010: 47). In Joshua, the particular kind of myth (among several kinds that Earl identifies) lies within a theological framework, so that its influence on the community's self-understanding relates especially to its response to God. One of the features of a myth of this kind is that it locates the story of the people in 'foundational' or 'prototypical' time (Earl 2010: 47) and, therefore, in Joshua's case, the time of Israel's origins in its land. Its interest in this subject is explained by its character as a 'mythical' explanation of Israel's existence.

We have already observed some of the features of Joshua that might be called 'mythic'. The historical time that the book refers to shades over into the primaeval time of creation. This becomes evident in several places. The first is the crossing of the Jordan itself, with its echoes of the crossing of the Reed Sea on the journey out of Egypt. These two episodes have significance beyond the fording of bodies of water, calling to mind the primordial battles between the god of order and the 'Sea' as a manifestation of Chaos in ancient Near Eastern creation stories. The word *yām* is both the ordinary name for 'sea' and the name of the Canaanite god Yam, overcome by Baal in the Ugaritic tale of Baal's supremacy and this echo is clear in a text like Ps. 74.13-14 (cf. Exod. 15.1). The same text uses other names for the Chaos monster, namely Leviathan (resembling the name *ltn* found in texts from the city of Ugarit, on the Phoenician coast, in the second millennium BCE) or simply the 'dragons'. In another place it is Rahab (Ps. 89.10 [MT 11] – not the same as Rahab the prostitute); or Tiamat, destroyed by Marduk in the Babylonian story, and sometimes thought to have a resonance with the Hebrew *tᵉhôm*, 'the deep', as in Gen. 1.2 or Exod. 15.5. The 'crossing' of the Jordan, therefore, that important motif in the early chapters of the book, symbolizes the prevailing of the power to order over a power that tends to disorder.

A second example of the shading over of history into myth is the record of the annihilation of the Anakim in Josh. 11.21-23 (cf. Deut. 9.2). These were a larger-than-life people, the ancestors of another giant race, the Nephilim (Num. 13.33), who in turn are said to have roamed the earth in the primaeval time when 'the sons of God' commingled with 'the daughters of humans', with unnatural results (Gen. 6.1, 4). That the enemies of Israel are typified by this gigantic, primordial people at the point where Joshua is said to have totally subjugated the land of Canaan, lifts the significance of the conflict beyond the level of the historical.

A third feature of this sort is Joshua 18.1, where, as we have already observed, the subjugation of the 'land' has echoes of the creational mandate to 'subdue the earth' (Gen. 1.28). The ambivalence of the Hebrew *'ereṣ* as both 'land' and 'earth' is exploited by this intertextual echo to suggest, once more, that the narrative in Joshua has a greater significance than an account of the possession of a territory.

We saw in Younger's analysis of conquest accounts that behind them generally lay a deep concern for the re-establishment of 'order' in the world, where 'order' was conceived according to the world-view of the writers. Joshua too is concerned with the true ordering of the world, that is, by the sovereign decree of Yahweh, who determined the destinies of nations. Torah and covenant were central to the expression of such order. But the echoes of primaeval time and creational purpose convey that the order in question is not just historical or political, but also natural and cosmic. It might be objected to this that the Old Testament, in Exodus and Joshua, turns the creation-nature orientation of the ancient Near Eastern myths into a more 'historical' conception of the deity's relationship to the world. But the idea of a sharp distinction between Israel and its neighbours in this regard is no longer as widely held as it once was. (Key references are Schmid 1984 and Brueggemann 1997: 159-64).

In the conflict in Canaan, the most fundamental issues of existence are played out. Jericho is not just the oasis-city, located at a strategically crucial cross-roads, but stands symbolically for the chaotic evil that opposes God's benevolent ordering of the world. The picture of it, shut up against Israel, seems to stand for a kind of opposition to God's project with Israel that is not merely human or military. This is no ordinary battle-account, for the people of the city do not take up arms, and on Israel's side it is God who conquers. The 'conquest' of Canaan is emblematic of the fulfilment of God's mandate to human beings at the creation to 'subdue the earth', that is, to govern it in such a way as to achieve God's most profound desire and purpose for it. Joshua's conquest of Canaan is *merely* an emblem of this, because it is situated within the contingencies of history, politics and nature, with all their evidently unfinished business. The narrative is therefore 'eschatological', in the sense that it points beyond itself to an unrealized time, when God's rule will be established in a thoroughgoing way.

A reading of Joshua as myth in this sense enables a search for meaning beyond the level of bloodshed and xenophobia, as Earl has it, and expresses a deep desire for 'rest' (Earl 2010: 47). This 'rest', however, does not come without conflict, represented by the wars in Joshua. Israel's war with Canaan, therefore, is a function of God's war with everything that opposes the creative, ordering purpose of God. Such opposition may derive ultimately from powers in heaven, but it also plays out on earth. The conflict with Canaan, as a symbol of God's war with all opposition to his will, is not removed from the historical and political sphere, but includes it. This is not to say that God's conflict with opposition is simply to be played out in wars between Israel and Canaan. Rather, it means that the divine purpose to create an order in the world finds one of its expressions in the political, cultural and moral life of nations. The war with Canaan, in Deuteronomy and Joshua, may be seen as a kind of 'culture-critique', which involves not only the war with Canaan, but the entire programme laid out in Deuteronomy for a nation governed by Torah. (For examples of how this may be understood, see Goldingay 1987: 59-96; Wright 1996: 8-17).

This is the context in which the concept of *ḥērem*, or command of total destruction, is best understood. That is, it is a figurative expression of the radical distinction between a communal life organized around the divine will, as expressed in Torah, and all other kinds of communal life (cf. Earl 2010: 63; Macdonald 2003: 113-23).

This discussion of Joshua as 'myth', expressing aspects of Israelite identity and containing a kind of culture-critique over against 'Canaan', does not in itself answer the question when and for what particular reasons the book may have been written. It is compatible with proposals for dating the book that we have encountered in Chapter 2, namely as part of Israel's attempt to understand its ethnically and religiously mixed situation in the late monarchy or after the exile. In such a case, 'Canaanites' may stand for non-Yahwists living alongside Yahwists in the land.

Further Approaches to Meaning-Making

The discussion of myth in Joshua has opened up the possibility of understanding its rhetoric of violence in ways that depart from the literal or surface meaning of the texts. This enables many approaches to be explored. In one such approach, L. Rowlett offers a particular interpretation of the violent rhetoric of Joshua in terms of identity, in which she sees it as legitimating a certain power-structure within monarchic Israel. That is, applying Michel Foucault's philosophy of power, she argues that the rhetoric of violence intends to persuade its audience to accept the centralizing ideology in the reform of King Josiah, with the implication of the ascendancy of forces of social control in the royal elite in Jerusalem (Rowlett 1996, e.g. p. 15). She is thus close to the strand in scholarship on Old Testament history often known as 'minimalist', in which the apparently historical texts of the Old Testament convey relatively little about the ancient past, but belong to a programme to promote the interests of a ruling elite in the post-exilic Persian province of Yehud (e.g. Davies 1992). This is a kind of understanding of 'history' in which history is written to justify certain structures of power.

W. Brueggemann, somewhat differently, bases his analysis of Joshua's violent language more broadly on the hermeneutical axiom that readers participate in the making of meaning. He combines this with a theological understanding of the canon of Scripture, according to which it 'provides materials for ongoing disputatious interpretation' (Brueggemann 2009: 10). This resolves into a belief that the theological concept of divine revelation cannot be understood apart from 'social process' (p. 26). He takes as a reference point Josh. 11.4, in which God instructs Joshua to hamstring the horses of the king of Hazor, but puts in question the notion that God is thereby revealed as having commanded the violent destruction of the people of the city. Rather, to try to convey a nuanced argument briefly, horses and chariots represent, in sociological perspective, the forces of monarchical tyranny and oppression; Yahweh is known, theologically, to be a God of liberation from oppression, and therefore it is outside the conceptual capacity of the community of Joshua that this can occur without violent action. Joshua is to be understood as 'liberation narratives' (p. 49), that is, in the context of the Old Testament's canonical literature of liberation. Brueggemann finally, wants to provoke a reading of Joshua's violence that discerns between the underlying theological truths of justice and liberation and the language of violence, so as to facilitate a modern reading of the book in a way that enables a critique of militarism.

The point shows that various methodological approaches may yield quite different accounts of what Joshua 'is'. Brueggemann's reading will have a bearing on the next chapter and, more particularly, on our final chapter on the history of the use of the book and its continued use today.

Conclusion

The book of Joshua conforms in important respects to a form of writing that can be classified as ancient conquest accounts. This implies that it understands itself as giving an account of history. But this must be qualified by saying that what counts as history-writing varies according to the norms and expectations of cultures. A recognition of this can explain, for example, why apparently discrepant versions of Joshua's campaign can exist side by side and suggest that modern explanations of such discrepancies by appeal to different sources' perspectives are unnecessary. Even so, Joshua's picture of Israel's foundational history has certain figurative and symbolic aspects, which means that the book as 'history' does not substitute for modern enquiries into the history of the period and places to which it refers. It also poses fundamental philosophical questions about the nature of history and why it is written.

The category of myth was found to be helpful for understanding the way in which Joshua might have served to express some of the deepest aspects of Israel's self-understanding as the people of God. It made possible an appropriation of the violence of the book, including the concept of the *ḥērem*, in such a way as not to take it as a paradigm for violent action. On the contrary, it helped towards an understanding of the book as having an eschatological horizon, in which the surface-level referents of the text pointed to greater and deeper realities. And this in turn opens the way to theological appropriations which may be described as typological or spiritual. In other words, it is a pre-requisite of theological readings whose horizons are the bigger biblical picture, and in Christian appropriation, Christological. Such readings are not, therefore, necessarily fanciful, but take their cue from signals within the text of Joshua itself.

Bibliography

Aharoni, Y. *The Land of the Bible: A Historical Geography* (London: Burns & Oates, 1962).

Albright, W.F. *Yahweh and the Gods of Canaan* (New York: Doubleday, 1968).

Bienkowski, P. *Jericho in the Late Bronze Age* (Warminster: Aris & Philips, 1986).

Bimson, J.J. *Redating the Exodus and Conquest* (JSOTSup, 5; Sheffield: Almond Press, 2nd edn, 1981).

– 'The Origins of Israel in Canaan: An Examination of Recent Theories', *Themelios* 15.1 (1989), pp. 4-15.

Bright, John. *A History of Israel* (Philadelphia, PA: Westminster Press, 3rd edn, 1981).

Brueggemann, W. *Divine Presence amid Violence: Contextualizing the Book of Joshua* (Milton Keynes: Paternoster; Eugene, OR: Cascade Books, 2009).

– *Theology of the Old Testament: Testimony, Dispute, Advocacy* (Minneapolis, MN: Fortress Press, 1997).

Davies, Philip R. *In Search of 'Ancient Israel'* (JSOTSup, 148; Sheffield: Sheffield Academic Press, 1992, 1995).

Earl, Douglas S. *Reading Joshua as Christian Scripture* (JTISup, 2; Winona Lake, IN: Eisenbrauns, 2010).

– *The Joshua Delusion: Rethinking Genocide in the Bible* (Eugene, OR: Cascade Books, 2010).

Finkelstein, I. *The Archaeology of the Israelite Settlement* (Jerusalem: Israel Exploration Society, 1988).

Goldingay, John E. *Theological Diversity and the Authority of the Old Testament* (Grand Rapids, MI: Eerdmans, 1987).

Gottwald, N. *The Tribes of Yahweh* (Maryknoll, NY: Orbis, 1979).

Kallai, Zecharia. *Biblical Historiography and Historical Geography* (BEATAJ, 44; Frankfurt: Peter Lang, 1998).

Kenyon, Kathleen. *Digging Up Jericho: The Results of the Jericho Excavations 1952–1956* (New York: Praeger, 1957).

Kitchen, K.A. *The Bible in its World* (Downers Grove, IL: IVP, 1977).

MacDonald, Nathan. *Deuteronomy and the Meaning of Monotheism* (FAT, 2/1; Tübingen: Mohr Siebeck, 2003).

Mazar, Amihai. 'The Iron Age I', in A. Ben-Tor (ed.), *The Archaeology of Ancient Israel* (New Haven and London: Yale University Press and the Open University of Israel, 1992), pp. 258-301.

Na'aman, N. 'The Law of the Altar in Deuteronomy and the Cultic Site near Shechem', in S.L. McKenzie and T. Römer (eds.), *Rethinking the Foundations: Historiography in the Ancient World and in the Bible: Essays in Honour of John Van Seters* (BZAW, 294; Berlin, New York: de Gruyter, 2000), pp. 141-61.

Noth, M. *The History of Israel* (trans. P.R. Ackroyd; New York: Harper & Row, second edn, 1960).

Rowlett, L. *Joshua and the Rhetoric of Violence: A New Historicist Analysis* (JSOTSup, 226; Sheffield: Sheffield Academic Press, 1996).

Schmid, H.H. 'Creation, Righteousness and Salvation: "Creation Theology" as the Broad Horizon of Biblical Theology', in Bernhard W. Anderson (ed.), *Creation in the Old Testament* (Philadelphia: Fortress Press; London: SPCK, 1984).

Van Seters, John. *In Search of History: Historiography in the Ancient World and the Origins of Biblical History* (New Haven and London: Yale University Press, 1983).

Wright, C.J. *Deuteronomy* (NIBC; Peabody, MA: Hendrickson, 1996).

Younger, K. Lawson. *Ancient Conquest Accounts: A Study in Ancient Near Eastern and Biblical History Writing* (JSOTSup, 98; Sheffield: Sheffield Academic Press, 1990).

5

Joshua and Theology

Hermeneutics of a Theology of Joshua

The aim of the present chapter is to articulate the theology of the book of Joshua. This is the most complicated, contentious and important task we face in our attempt to understand it. The theological question is an intrinsic part of the book's interpretation, simply because its subject-matter concerns God and God's relationships with human beings. Furthermore, the book forms part of the canons of faith-communities, both Jewish and Christian, and it is very unlikely that we would even possess it if that were not the case. The book has, of course, literary, historical and sociological aspects, and no doubt others, all of which are valid forms of enquiry in themselves. Yet none of them can be isolated, in the end, from the theological enquiry, since all will relate in some sense to the essential question about the ways in which Joshua makes claims to offer a true account of reality.

Having said that, the topic of the 'theology of Joshua' can mean different things. It could mean the kind of question framed by a believing community: what does the book of Joshua invite us to believe about God? This might be called a question in Systematic or Doctrinal Theology? Or in terms of what might be called 'biblical theology', it could be put slightly differently, as what is specific to Joshua within the broad context of the theology of the Bible. Or at a yet further remove from the existential question of the believing community, it might simply aim to describe what the supposed writers of Joshua believed about God.

The book of Joshua does, in fact, play a part in regulating the beliefs of communities. One outstanding example of this is the way in which it affects the politics of Israel-Palestine. That will be taken up as a special topic in the following chapter, when we will look at the ways in which the book has actually been interpreted and applied. In the present chapter, we will consider how to approach the theology of Joshua more generally, with some attention to each of the forms of the question just outlined (though we will not organize the treatment in that way).

History

The essential preliminary to the theological question is how to articulate what the book actually says. All the preceding chapters have aimed to help us do this. They have also shown, however, that the attempt is contentious at every point. The historical question (Chapter 4) matters because the way in which one answers it has implications for the way in which the surface narrative relates to external reality. If the book was composed close to the events and tells a story that corresponds somewhat closely to 'what actually happened', the likely corollary is that the language of the book should be taken in a plain sense. That is, it intends to say that God really did command Joshua to exterminate the Canaanites in order to possess their land. In that case, an estimate of the justice of God, the way in which God works in history, the meaning of the election of Israel, and of course, the *ḥērem* enacted on Canaan, will be developed on the assumption that this is true. The strength of this position (represented in a number of commentaries referenced in the present volume) is the 'historical' nature of the kind of faith attested in the Bible. God is known in Israel by the 'signs and wonders' by which he brought the people out of Egypt (Deut. 4.34). The belief that God does or can act powerfully in history for salvation is at home in both Jewish and Christian theology. In the former it finds expression, for example, in the Passover service, with its memory of God's past saving acts and also its future hope, summed up in the words; 'Next year in Jerusalem'. In the latter, God is known above all in the life, death and resurrection of Jesus Christ. Scripture testifies to these things. The book of Joshua apparently testifies to a particular phase of this biblical 'salvation-history', the piece of the story of Israel that explains how it came to inhabit the land in which its life before Yahweh was played out. The case for reading Joshua thus (accurate at least in respect of a 'core' of what it claims) has been put cogently by Stephen Williams, albeit with a concession that it is possible to affirm the historic Christian faith while allowing that the establishment of the historicity of Joshua is subject to various kinds of enquiry (McConville and Williams 2010: 207-14, and note 209-10). He writes: 'If this is fiction, ideology, or whatever without real basis in fact, the grounds for Israel's claim to know God, as testimony is borne to it in the Old Testament, are surely removed to a significant degree' (p. 212).

However, this was the topic where the authors (McConville and Williams) offered the reader different ways of looking at it. For my part, I indicated the several different takes on Israel's history contained in the Old Testament (e.g. Samuel–Kings and Chronicles), which arose in different historical situations, each presumably with their own purposes. This being so, Old Testament history might be '…a bringing to bear of a stream of tradition on a present exigency, with the prophetic purposes of reproach, warning, encouragement, and renewal of vision' (pp. 230-35 [232]). The issue, I think, is not whether God has acted in history, but in what ways Scripture testifies to this. It is a matter of theological hermeneutics and the range of scholarly theological work on Joshua shows that there are simply different approaches to this. (See also Earl 2010: esp. 1-14). If one thinks the narrative of Joshua is only loosely related to the events purportedly described, then it may relate to history by bringing to bear memories of ancient traditions on contemporary problems. Possibilities of symbolic and metaphorical language are opened up and this, in turn, has implications for the ways in which God may be held to act in history, to have chosen Israel and to come in grace and judgment.

Literature

A second aspect of the question as to what Joshua actually says is the literary one, as addressed above in chaps. 2 and 3. The challenge, in this case, is where to locate the 'voice' of the book of Joshua. We saw that traditional literary-critical approaches tended to discern different voices which could be aligned with the tendencies of sources or redactions, such as Deuteronomic or Priestly. A 'theological' reading of Joshua, in these terms, could become a description of competing points of view, layered into a growing body of literature that eventually becomes Joshua. The book could also become a jig-saw piece in a larger puzzle in which theological interpretations are sought for Deuteronomy–Kings (the Deuteronomistic History, DtrH), Genesis–Joshua (Hexateuch) or even Genesis–Kings. Such an approach makes it difficult to articulate a 'theology of Joshua' because this seems open to endless modification or correction.

Dissatisfied with both the methodology and outcomes of redactional approaches, another kind of literary approach (Chapter 3) sought the 'voice' of Joshua in the texture of the book as a whole. Surface tensions could now become functions of the meaning of the book. The claims about total conquest points up ironically the actual compromises made by Joshua and Israel. The characterization of the Canaanites as coming under judgment for their hardness of heart (Josh. 11.20) recalls that Israel itself has been portrayed exactly in this way (Deut. 9. 4-6) and that this was the very ground of God's action towards them in mercy and grace (Polzin 1980: 87-88). Polzin thus insists on finding the theological meaning of Joshua not in putative sources or redactions, which may impose inappropriate templates on interpretation, but in the unique discourse of the book itself and the complex interrelationship of its parts.

Constituents of the Theology of Joshua

A further dimension of what the book of Joshua actually says theologically consists in the expressly theological themes that are part and parcel of its substance. Such themes are recognizable in Joshua because they are drawn from the wider biblical story of which Joshua forms a part. They include the worship of Yahweh alone, creation, covenant, law, grace, judgment and land. (These are addressed by Williams 2010: 93-170. His list of topics is shorter, but in practice he deals with all of these). As with literary analysis, there is a danger of being distracted from Joshua by the possible meanings of sources or redactions, so it is with theological themes. One can, of course, attempt to describe the Old Testament's theology of covenant by considering all the strands that contribute to it. But not everything that can be said about covenant will be found in the book of Joshua on the subject. One of the assumptions of the literary- or redactional-critical type of enquiry, indeed, is that that there may be different conceptions of a topic like covenant within individual sources or redactions. So our immediate question is what kind of inflection does the book of Joshua give to each theological topic. This might be somewhat reversed to ask how the book of Joshua adopts or adapts theological tradition for the purpose of its message? An extension of the question would be how Joshua on covenant is taken up, developed, or indeed surpassed or negated in other parts of the Scriptures of the Old and New Testaments (a direction taken by Williams 2010).

With this in mind, we turn now to consider some of the theological themes that appear in the book.

Idolatry and 'Yahweh Alone'

The book of Joshua is driven by the logic of the First Commandment of the Decalogue (Exod. 20.3; Deut. 5.7) with its call to worship Yahweh alone and its obverse in the prohibition of the worship of 'other gods' (Josh. 24.43). In Deuteronomy, where this commandment is developed at length theologically (Deuteronomy 5–11), the destruction of places of worship dedicated to other gods is at the heart of its programme for Israel's possession of the promised land (Deut. 12.1-7). The command to worship Yahweh alone also undergirds all the important features of Joshua: the gift of the land to Israel, the requirement of obedience to the Torah given through Moses (1.8), the concept of Israel organized both liturgically and militarily around the ark of the covenant on its procession into the land (chaps. 3–6), the assumption of Yahweh's unchallenged power in nature (10.12-14) and history, the celebration of Passover as a first act in the newly gifted land (5.10-12), the covenant ceremonies at Ebal (8.30-35) and Shechem (chap. 24), the apparent challenge to the exclusive worship of Yahweh in the confrontation with the Transjordanians in chap. 22 and, of course, the application of the *ḥērem* to the population of Canaan.

The book may therefore be said to stage, in narrative form, a fundamental conflict between the worship of Yahweh alone and every other ultimate allegiance, which is therefore idolatry. (It is interesting that Joshua tends to target the 'kings' of Canaan as symbolic of radical opposition to the project of Yahweh, notably in chap. 12). This uncompromising view of God is at the root of the problem that the book poses to many modern readers. The Bible's 'monotheism' (a term which should be used only in a qualified way about biblical religion) has been severely criticized. Jan Assmann sees it as inherently oppressive and exclusive and contrasts it unfavourably with the 'inclusive', polytheistic religion of Egypt (Assmann 1997). And Regina Schwartz believes it has left a 'violent legacy' in cultures influenced by the Bible (Schwartz 1997). In some recent scholarship on Israel's religious history, monotheism is depicted as a late revision of the past intended to repudiate diversity (e.g. Gnuse 1997). These views have been criticized in turn, not least for the claimed correlation between polytheistic forms of religion and the virtues of tolerance and inclusion. N. Lohfink firmly rejects a specific claim of Assmann about violent monotheism: 'I find this sentence in itself to be an act of violence' (Lohfink 2005: 149, author's translation; see further in McConville 2006: 19-20). The exchange is symptomatic of the powerful feelings engendered by the topic. Richard Bauckham has also challenged the notion of monotheism as a late development in Israel (Bauckham 2004).

The Old Testament's adherence to a belief in 'Yahweh alone' can be viewed more positively, as an engine of 'cultural critique', especially of religious-political systems like ancient Assyria and their ideological dependence on perpetual war (Otto 1999; McConville 2006: 20-29). Such an appraisal can be expressed so as to extend to Joshua. The argument for 'Yahweh alone' as cultural critique depends on the supposition that life in loyalty and obedience to Yahweh is infinitely better than life under any other ultimate commitment. For Williams, the call to worship Yahweh alone implies that that is the only way to live in accordance with reality. Idolatry is correspondingly dangerous, both to society – 'the whole of social life unravels when idolatry is practiced' (Williams, p. 131) – and to the individual's personality (p. 135). The claims of 'Yahweh alone' extend to all aspects of existence, including the aesthetic. Idolatry has lost sight of the *beauty* of God (pp. 137-39). And he recalls Nietzsche's rejection of Christianity on the grounds of *taste* (p. 139).

Covenant and Israel

Closely associated with the command to worship Yahweh alone in Joshua is the theme of Yahweh's covenantal relationship with Israel. The story of covenant, in the narrative prior to Joshua, embraces the ancient promises to the patriarchs, primarily built around land and nationhood (Gen. 12.1-3; 15.17-21) and the Mosaic covenant at Sinai, characterized by Torah (Exodus 19–24; Deuteronomy 4–5). The story singles out Israel for the special privilege of a close relationship with the God who, at the same time, claims to be the God of the whole earth. On the face of it, this seems to support the idea of an excluding God, portrayed by Assmann and others.

However, as we have seen, the definition of Israel is turned into a conundrum by the nexus of Rahab, Achan and the Gibeonites, a dominant thread in the narrative of chaps. 1–12. Israel as an indivisible unity and as an ethnic identity is subverted by these stories. Some of those who thought they were properly Israelite turn out not to be, and others who had apparently no such claim find that they take their place within the people. (The Gibeonites have a rather second-rate citizenship, but Rahab's position seems to carry no such inhibition.) The ironies of this narrative, observed in Chapter 3, have a powerful theological message, namely that Israel is defined not by absolute right of inheritance, but by actual allegiance to Yahweh. The point is reinforced by Joshua's rhetoric in the covenant-renewal at Shechem, when he declares: 'You cannot serve Yahweh' (24.19), an extreme statement of the fact that Israel had no natural or permanent right to a special relationship with Yahweh. The tenor of the story of election and covenant in Joshua is thus, very clearly, that where Canaan goes today, Israel could go tomorrow.

It is in this connection that Torah plays a part in the theology of the book. Joshua is charged at the outset with keeping Torah (1.8), and the nation that is worthy of the name of Israel will be one that does so. The narrative presents a rather uneven picture of the success of Joshua and the leaders of Israel in doing so. There is no simple correlation between the pattern they set and the kind of behaviour held out for imitation. Once again, the Rahab episode and the irresolute handling of the Gibeonites testify to this. (Here, the reader is asked to accept, for the purposes of the appraisal of the characters, that what Yahweh commands is good, though the sense in which some of the commands in Joshua may be 'good' is one of our current questions.) Yet in one traceable narrative line, Joshua has the status of a worthy successor to Moses, such that he has been thought to foreshadow King Josiah, the paradigm of a righteous king in the books of Kings (Nelson 1981). When he takes the lead in covenant-renewal at Shechem and declares that he and his house will serve Yahweh (24.15c) whatever anyone else does, we have no reason to read this suspiciously. The most convincing evidence of Joshua's integrity, in my view, is that he ultimately accepts a limited role for himself in his succession to Moses. This runs counter to narratives of power practically everywhere else in the Old Testament. Far from seeking the mantle of kingship, Joshua simply retires, his work done, to his inheritance in a corner of Ephraim (19.50; 24.29-30). He is, in this respect, a model of self-effacing service and of what Torah-obedience might look like in practice.

Land

The land is an inescapable part of any description of the theology of Joshua. One of the arguments for a 'Hexateuch' was that Joshua supplied the story of land-occupation that was conspicuously missing from the Pentateuch. Land was promised to Abraham (Gen. 12.1-3) and the theology of Yahweh's gift of land to Israel was expressed profoundly in Deuteronomy. The gift of land to Israel in Joshua is a correlative of the command to worship Yahweh alone and to keep his covenant.

The land in Joshua has a certain objective reference. It is described internally and externally by border-descriptions and city-lists and corresponds, in some measure, to the physical space in which the people known as Israel had their historical existence. Yet, as we saw in earlier chapters, there is something curiously under-determined about the definition of the land. The internal tribal divisions shifted. The status of the Jordan as a boundary was a recurring question. And the concept of the land as extending from the far north to the southern extremities gave some signs of being theoretical, as far as the northern reaches were concerned. As Curtis has it, the picture of the land in Joshua 'is ideal rather than real' (Curtis 1994: 75). We have just observed about the people of Israel that it resisted definition in a permanent, objective way, and the same appears to be true about the land.

The point about the land is precisely that it is a gift and part of the constellation of elements that make up the picture of life lived well before God in Joshua. The land, though it has a real existence as actual land, is also a symbol of 'the good life' in the sense of the life that belongs within the divine purpose for the whole creation. The semantic fusion of 'land' and 'earth', not only in Joshua but elsewhere in the Old Testament, has been commented on a number of times above, especially in the key text Josh. 18.1. The narrative of Joshua regarding land has Old Testament intertexts in, for example, Lev. 25.23 ('...the land is mine, says Yahweh') and Ps. 24.1 ('The earth is Yahweh's, and its fullness'). The term used in all these texts is *'ereṣ*. 'Land'-theology has several aspects in the Old Testament, including its relationship with kinship and jubilee (Leviticus 25) and its inseparability from social justice (Amos 5.11), but the notion that land/earth is Yahweh's to give predominates in the theology of Joshua. It is also presented as a fundamental good in human experience. Land, therefore, corresponds to the theological theme of 'place' as an indispensable element in the 'good life' (see Bartholomew 2011; O'Donovan 1989).

The idea of Joshua as the story of God giving a land to Israel, therefore, has to be qualified in an important way, namely as an instance of God's creation-purpose to give land/earth to human beings. It is a case of land/earth 'made clean' in the sense of a consecration to its divinely ordained purpose (Williams, p. 103). At the same time it is a historical contingency. This appears both in the book of Joshua's resistance to an absolute and permanent definition of the land and in the conditionality of the covenant. The gift of land appears both as an accomplished act of God and as a continuing task (that paradox contained in the literary form of the book). The land that is given can also be lost, or at least must always continue to be taken. That is the theological implication of the unfinished business signalled in Josh. 13.1. It is not that the job just happened not to have been completed yet at the time of writing. It is of the essence of the portrayal of the gift of land that the business remains unfinished. This is not a mandate for continuous conquest in some literal sense, however, but a symbolic representation of the need to remain perpetually faithful to the covenant with Yahweh.

Williams puts a further telling slant on this. The great exception made for the tribe of Levi in Joshua's land-distribution is emblematic of the non-permanence, or non-absoluteness, of ancient Israel's possession of the land described in Joshua. For him, this is a function not just of the discourse of Joshua itself, but also of the New Testament prospect of 'a new inheritance, which is not that of earthly land, but something imperishably preserved in heaven (1 Pet. 1:4; 2:9)' (Williams, p. 107).

Yahweh-War, Ḥērem and 'Counter-Violence'

The pervading assumption of the book of Joshua is the possibility of the 'good life' in land created and given by Yahweh. The occupation of the land of Canaan by Israel is presented as a step towards the realization of such a possibility. The possibility comes in the form of covenantal obligation to live in the land under Torah, in faithfulness to Yahweh, for it is only such a life that can be called 'good'. The book of Joshua imagines a reality in which the people of Israel lives in gifted land in such a way as to fulfil the creation mandate to human beings to manage and enjoy the earth and the creatures in it (Gen. 1.28). This imagined reality encompasses moral, social and political dimensions of life, all as functions of the religious reality of the benevolent rule of Yahweh.

It also imagines the opposite, that is, a moral, political and social reality that honours other ultimate loyalties and, in its refusal of the worship of Yahweh, is characterized as idolatrous. This negative vision is projected through the city-states of Canaan, with Jericho's symbolic 'shutting up' against Israel as the parade example (Josh. 6.1). Theologically, the hostility of Canaan is of a piece with the profound antipathy of the Pharaoh of Exodus to the Yahweh-project of liberating a people to serve him, rather than Pharaoh himself (Exod. 1.10-14; 5.1-2; 8.1). The motif of the 'hardening of Pharaoh's heart' in Exodus (Exod. 8.15; 11.10; cf. 14.17) is replicated in Joshua and applied to the Canaanites as a whole (Josh. 11.20). The story from Exodus to Joshua cannot be understood in its own terms apart from this moral-spiritual conflict. And this is the context of the themes in Joshua of the *ḥērem*, or command of utter destruction, and the Yahweh-war against Canaan.

The war against Canaan has often been understood as a 'holy war', that is, that it had the character, in some sense, of an act of worship. It might find support in the Deuteronomic distinction between wars fought within the land given to Israel, in which the *ḥērem* was to operate, and wars fought outside its boundaries (Deut. 20.10-18). However, evidence for a specifically cultic or liturgical kind of war, as opposed to other kinds, is thin, since all wars in ancient Israel's time, like all of life, were conducted under the aegis of God. This is illustrated by the role of the priest in encouraging the armies of Israel before going on any military campaign (Deut. 20.2), exhorting to faith and obedience to Yahweh in this particular context, just as in all areas of life (Deut. 6.5-9). Other nations had a similarly religious view of war, as evidenced, for example, by the Moabite Mesha Inscription (Nelson *Joshua*, 1997: 17). It is probably better, therefore, to think of 'the wars of Yahweh' in general, rather than a special kind of Holy War (see also Curtis 1994: 76-77).

As the war in Joshua is not by definition an act of worship, so the *ḥērem* should not be understood as a 'sacrifice', in spite of the command to kill the human population (and, in Jericho's case, the livestock, too). It is better, with Nelson, to see it as putting the persons and goods of a conquered city beyond human use, on the grounds that they belonged to God alone (even persons could be traded as slaves; Nelson *Joshua*, 1997: 19-20; also 'Ḥerem', 1997).

This much is to try to clarify the concepts of Yahweh-war and *ḥērem*. That is different from saying how they function theologically in Joshua. In the preceding chapter, we saw reasons to regard a number of aspects of Joshua as symbolic and so to think of the work as 'mythic'. That is, its meaning lay not on the surface of the narrative, but in its capacity to engage the imagination of its audience so that it shaped their view of themselves,

God and the world. The *ḥērem*, on this view, is a symbolic instrument of the culture critique, or rigorous reprobation of idolatry, outlined above.

Once it is accepted that the *ḥērem* should be interpreted symbolically or metaphorically, within a mythic conception of the meaning of Joshua, it remains to ask in what sense this may have been received and understood by an audience. What is the theological cash-value? It has been described as 'a metaphor for religious fidelity' (Moberly 1999: 135). MacDonald specifies it further as 'radical obedience to YHWH's command, as the absence of "abomination", as something that must transcend human desires for wealth or family [and as indicating] the need for separation and the importance of education' (MacDonald 2003: 113-23, here p. 123). But a question remains about what happens to the meaning of the *ḥērem* when it has been separated from its literal sense of the physical destruction of people. Is what is involved in 'religious fidelity' therefore removed altogether from the sphere of history, nature and politics and into some 'spiritual' sphere that is, by definition, removed from these?

It is important to make a distinction between 'symbol' (or 'metaphor') on one hand and 'spiritualization' on the other. The reading of Joshua as 'culture-critique' implies that its relevance lies not merely in the inner being of individuals, but in the lives and values of communities in relation to each other. It is implausible to extract Joshua from the realms of the political and historical. Yet modern readers will be aware of the dangers of any reading of Joshua that could give an appearance of legitimacy to acts of war or violence.

Part of the answer to this dilemma in reading Joshua is to observe that, canonically, violence is portrayed as the essential mark of human sinfulness. This is evident in the opening chapters of Genesis in which violence (*ḥāmās*) especially characterizes the condition of humanity that led to the divine judgment of the flood (Gen. 6.11-13; Williams, p. 112). The canonical tendency of the Old Testament is towards a kingdom of peace (e.g. Isa. 9.6-7 [MT 5-6]; 11.6-9), and thus to the overcoming of violence itself. Joshua may be said to participate in this forward movement by virtue of its creational and eschatological orientation that we have observed already. This aspect of the book's theology is exemplified in the glimpse of the creation ideal contained in Josh. 18.1. And we saw how the narrative of the conquest of Jericho drew imaginatively on the concept of Jubilee, so as to depict that event in terms of both creation and liberation (above, Chapter 3) – the note that was also struck in the words of the Spiritual cited in the Introduction. When we read Joshua as part of a deeply compromised human history that is (theologically-speaking) on the way to redemption into a divine kingdom of peace, we make room for the sense that the things done in Joshua are wrong and should not be done, and yet that the book joins in a testimony to the renewal of all things. There is thus a distinction, in O'Donovan's terms, between 'moral ends' and 'historical ends' (O'Donovan 1994: 156-59). It is important to emphasize that this is an affirmation of the Old Testament's witness to divine presence and action in history. The point can be made both within an Old Testament context (where the prophets furnish numerous images of renewal and peace) and in that of the Christian Bible. Christian readings that 'spiritualize' the Old Testament, or that otherwise tend to be Marcionite, can have the consequence, in practice, of becoming anti-Jewish. (Marcion was a second-century Christian who wanted the Church to abandon the Old Testament because he thought it presented a quite different and inferior understanding of God from the God who was revealed in Christ. He also tried to purge the New Testament of parts that were closely dependent on Old Testament history, such as the Gospels' infancy narratives. His teachings were rejected by the mainstream Church.) The attempt to read the Old Testament historically in a way that affirms its Jewishness, yet in the light of a Christian (Messianic) view is well exemplified by O'Donovan:

> Such a belief [i.e. Messianic], Christians have generally maintained against the Marcionite and anti-Jewish strands of thought in the church, does not imply disbelief in the amoral disclosures of God by ritual, cult and violence; but neither does it imply the permanence of the contingent social institutions of the Jewish past which have given expression to the moral order. It means that Christ turns these fragmentary utterances of God's voice, in warrior triumphs and legislative order, into a history which culminates in a divine manifestation and vindication of created order (1994: 159).

In practice, this also means that Joshua should be brought to bear on historical situations in such a way as to promote peace, not war. This will be one of our themes in the following chapter.

Bibliography

Assmann, J. *Moses the Egyptian: The Memory of Egypt in Western Monotheism* (Cambridge, MA: Harvard University Press, 1997).

Bartholomew, Craig. *Where Mortals Dwell* (Grand Rapids, MI: Baker, 2011).

Bauckham, Richard. 'Biblical Theology and the Problems of Monotheism', in C. Bartholomew *et al.* (eds.), *Out of Egypt: Biblical Theology and Biblical Interpretation* (SHS, 5; Carlisle: Paternoster; Grand Rapids, MI: Zondervan, 2004).

Earl, Douglas S. *The Joshua Delusion: Rethinking Genocide in the Bible* (Eugene, OR: Cascade Books, 2010).

Gnuse, R. *No Other Gods: Emergent Monotheism in Israel* (JSOTSup, 241; Sheffield: Sheffield Academic Press, 1997).

Lohfink, N. 'Gewalt und Monotheismus: Beispiel Altes Testament' *ThPQ* 153 (2005), pp. 149-62.

MacDonald, Nathan. *Deuteronomy and the Meaning of Monotheism* (FAT, 2/1; Tübingen: Mohr Siebeck, 2003).

McConville, J.G. *God and Earthly Power: An Old Testament Political Theology* (London: T. & T. Clark International, 2006, 2008).

Moberly, R.W.L. 'Toward an Interpretation of the Shema', in C. Seitz and K. Greene-McCreight (eds.), *Theological Exegesis: Essays in Honor of Brevard S. Childs* (Grand Rapids, MI: Eerdmans, 1999), pp. 124-44.

Nelson, R.D. 'Ḥerem and the Deuteronomic Social Conscience', in M. Vervenne and J. Lust (eds.), *Deuteronomy and Deuteronomic Literature* (BETL, 133; Leuven: Leuven University Press, 1997), pp. 39-54.

– 'Josiah in the Book of Joshua', *JBL* 100 (1981), pp. 531-40.

O'Donovan, Oliver. *Resurrection and the Moral Order* (Leicester: Apollos; Grand Rapids, MI: Eerdmans, 2nd edn, 1994).

– 'The Loss of a Sense of Place', *Irish Theological Quarterly* 55 (1989), pp. 39-58.

Otto, E. *Krieg und Frieden in der hebräischen Bible und im alten Orient* (Theologie und Frieden, 18; Stuttgart: Kohlhammer, 1999).

Schwartz, Regina. *The Curse of Cain: The Violent Legacy of Monotheism* (Chicago and London: Chicago University Press, 1997).

6

JOSHUA TODAY

Our final question is how the book of Joshua might be said to have relevance in the modern world. Within Christian and Jewish communities of faith it has the status of Scripture and this entails an attempt to understand how it might function as such. In that context, the question is not only about how it might have authority today, but also about how it is actually used and what kind of effect it has had on generations past and present. When we have considered that, it will be possible to evaluate whether it may still have something useful to say.

Not only in the public sphere at large, but also within believing communities, there is scepticism about whether Joshua can be reconciled with commonly held moral values. This is because it apparently legitimates a kind of warfare, and merciless violence within it, that looks to us like genocide or 'ethnic cleansing'. In the present chapter, we will look more closely at these things.

Theologically speaking, in our approach to Joshua, we may feel we are between a Scylla and Charybdis: if we wish to retain a theology of God at work in history, do we thereby retain the legacy of the Old Testament's violence? Alternatively, if we radically reject the 'violent' Old Testament deity, do we then forgo the concept of God at work in history, politics and social ethics? In both these cases, there are potentially serious implications for Jewish and Christian belief.

In the preceding chapter, we considered ways of thinking theologically about this question. In what follows, however, we will think about the historical effect of Joshua in relation to it. We will pursue it first on a broad canvas. Then, secondly, we will turn to a specific modern issue that is inextricably related to the book of Joshua because of its theme of the possession by a people called Israel of a land which others also regard as their home. In modern Israel-Palestine, the premises of Joshua take on an extreme relevance and urgency.

Joshua and Political Theology

In the preceding chapters, we have considered how the warlike aspects of Joshua might be mitigated by a reading of the *ḥērem* as a kind of cultural critique. This allowed an interpretation that could, in principle, be extended beyond the confines of the issue of ancient Israel's possession of the land of Canaan and in ways that did not involve either land or war.

Yet the topic of land remains stubbornly inextricable from Joshua. While symbolic or metaphorical approaches to Joshua can be justified in their own terms, the book is, nevertheless, a story of land-possession in a wider Old Testament narrative. In that narrative, Israel's existence in a land is an indispensable topic, whether it involves possession and enjoyment, or loss and yearning for return. Land has been identified as a leading theme in Old Testament theology (Brueggemann 1997). Is it possible to think properly about land-possession today in relation to the narrative of land-possession and of war waged to secure it in Joshua?

In numerous Old Testament writings, Yahweh the God of Israel is portrayed as the creator of all the earth (Ps. 24.1) and the one who gives land to its peoples (Amos 9.7; Deut. 2.5, 19). The sovereignty of Yahweh in the distribution of land is an essential component of his rule in history, and, therefore, of his theological characterization. One influential treatment of these themes is that of O'Donovan (1996). For him, the biblical story of Israel had four key aspects: salvation, judgment (or 'judicial discrimination', *mišpāṭ* or *ṣᵉdāqâ*), possession (or 'community-possession', *naḥᵃlâ*), and praise or worship (O'Donovan 1996: 36, and see pp. 36-49). To put it differently, it is a story of a people in its land, under law (or Torah) and worshipping God. This analysis is interesting because it both affirms the possibility of legitimate land-possession in God's world and ties it irrevocably to law and ethics, as well as to the vital question of ultimate value. For O'Donovan, this biblical story, in which Joshua plays a key part, is vitally important for thinking about political ethics because it sets forth a model of righteous rule and recognizes that legitimacy derives ultimately from God.

The idea of biblical history providing models for political rule can also be considered in relation to post-biblical political history, for better or worse. The idea of Israel as a 'nation-state', chosen by God and constituted by covenant with him, has been expressly adopted by a number of the nations of Christendom, including England and the United States (see Smith 2003: 66-94; Grosby 2002: 221-34). The concept of nationhood in modern times has been held to imply 'sacred foundations', consisting of community, territory, history and destiny (Smith 1993: 31). These things lie deep in the cultural memory of peoples whose traditions have been shaped by the Bible. Certainly, a nation's self-conscious modelling on Israel could take the form of nationalism, with exclusive tendencies. Yet the 'Deuteronomic' strain could also yield values in nationhood that are widely held today, such as the rule of law, universal citizenship and the responsible use of power. For S.D. McBride, the Deuteronomic Torah is '...the archetype of modern western constitutionalism' (McBride 1987: 75-76). Deuteronomy's 'sovereignty of the people' (that is, in contrast to a tyrannical political system) has been likened to modern democracy (Crüsemann 1996: 246-47; see also McConville 2006: 84-98). The modern academic study of law has shown that modern legal concepts and instances have roots in biblical law (Burnside 2011).

These aspects of the reception-history of the Deuteronomic strain in the Old Testament should be taken into account as part of any attempt to consider how the 'historical books' of the Old Testament, including Joshua, have made an impact on modern life and thought.

Joshua and Religious Warfare

The other side of the legacy of Joshua and Deuteronomy is their implication in a long history of war and violence in the name of religion. The broad context for this has been the inseparability of religion and politics at least since Constantine's vision of a cross at the Battle of Milvian Bridge (312 CE). This led to the consolidation of his power as Roman Emperor and his decision to make Christianity the official religion of the Empire, with its consequence in a triangle of Christianity, statehood and warfare. The Old Testament narrative thus lent language and concepts to the project of waging war in the name of Christian empire. For example, Pope Urban II launched the First Crusade with a characterization of the Muslims of the Holy Land as 'Amalekites' (Jenkins 2011: 125). With the development of nation-states, especially in Protestantism, their readiness to adopt the mantle of 'Israel' led very often to extreme violence against populations that posed a threat to their security in what they saw as their God-given lands. Jenkins documents the theologizing of violence against kings and other enemies, often invoking 'Amalek' as the perpetual type of the enemies of God and his chosen people (Jenkins 2011: 127-28; and see Exod. 17.14-16), and Phinehas as the zealous hero who did not hold back from executing the sentence of death on such enemies (see Numbers 25; Jenkins 2011: 130, and also p. 160 for Jewish appropriations of this). These paradigms operated in the execution of the English King Charles I and the English Civil War, which was fed by sharply conflicting interpretations of the Old Testament's understanding of the manner in which authority derived from God in the kingdom. Cromwell's reading of the biblical paradigms extended to the logic of total extermination on the grounds of the dire consequences, according to the biblical story, of Israel's having failed to destroy the

Canaanites completely and of Saul's sparing of the Amalekite King Agag
(Jenkins 2011: 130-32). In Ireland, Catholics could easily take the role of
Canaanites and the entire population of the Irish town of Drogheda, for
example, paid the price. A similar doctrine of 'extirpation' was adopted in
America (Jenkins 2011: 133-35) and derivations of *ḥērem* and 'holy war'
were applied in South Africa against the black population as well as in the
German notion of *Vernichtung* (annihilation), also in Africa decades before
Nazism ((Jenkins 2011: 39-41). In all these cases, notions of ultimate value
were at play, deriving from the theology of Israel's election. But the possibility always existed for such a concept to legitimate the state in and of itself.
In the extreme case of Nazi Germany, the state arguably became the object
of 'worship', hence the severe critique of it by Dietrich Bonhoeffer (e.g.
Bonhoeffer 1956; cf. Burleigh 2006: 38-122).

Critiques of 'Violent' Monotheism

Since early in the Christian era, the biblical narrative and concepts have
come in for severe criticism, often levelled against the entire Old Testament
and its portrayal of God. This goes back, at least, to Marcion in the second
century and the powerful Gnostic form of Christianity that distinguished
radically between the God of the Old Testament and the God of the New
(Jenkins 2011: 171-74). The Church rejected Marcion and Gnosticism, and
some adherents of the latter, such as the Cathars of southern France, fell
victim to the fiery zeal of the Inquisition. In doing so, it affirmed the unity
of the biblical revelation and God's close involvement in human history.
But since the early modern period, there has been a general questioning
of religious authority and beliefs. And in that context, radical criticism of
the biblical narrative and its language continues in the contemporary world
because of a perception that it is irrevocably implicated in the bloody history outlined above. The critique has been directed at Mosaic monotheism
itself because it is thought to have given rise to a history of tyranny, oppression and violence (Schwartz 1997, Assmann 1997). And advocates of the
'new atheism', like Christopher Hitchens, often cite the violence of the Old
Testament as grounds against biblical religion (Hitchens 2007: 97-107).

Responding to the Joshua Legacy

What responses are available to this rather mixed legacy of the book of
Joshua and related Old Testament literature? In approaches in which the
concern to reject the violent legacy of Joshua prevails, the response tends
to be to bracket out the violent sections, as has often been done in liturgical readings of the Psalms. One scholarly form of this is to make a sharp

distinction between the 'Deuteronomic' strand of Old Testament thought (including Joshua) that emphasizes the election of Israel, with the exclusive and warlike associations of this, and the 'prophetic' parts of the Old Testament. The latter are perceived to be characterized by qualities such as justice and compassion and to tend away from election-theology and towards inclusiveness (Jewett and Laurence 2003). In a further variation, Jenkins has argued that religious practice varies greatly in the ways in which it relates to the religion's Scriptures and that, in regard to the violent texts of the Old Testament, many believers have, in effect, learned to forget them (Jenkins 2011: 182). In pursuing this line of thought, Jenkins highlights the tradition of moral criticism of religion that comes broadly from the Enlightenment (pp. 174-82). Is it the case that modern Christians and Jews are obliged to 'forget' parts of their Scriptures in order to hold to commonly accepted modern beliefs about human rights, 'natural law', the conduct of war and genocide (as Jenkins implies, p. 182; cf. p. 175)?

We noticed above a view that biblical thought had effects on the modern world that are not always appreciated, for example, in the rule of law, the right use of power and respect for the individual. The point extends to the notion of 'natural law'. While there are modern, non-theological forms of this, the concept has roots in Christian theology, linked especially with the idea of the 'image of God' and thus to 'the capacity for moral judgment found in all men and women' (Porter 1999: 17). This calls into question the idea that biblical thought should be sharply contrasted with commonly held modern values. (For a penetrating analysis of the legacy of biblical and theological concepts in the modern world, see Taylor 2007). The book of Joshua is an integral part of a biblical theology of nationhood, sharing with Deuteronomy a basic paradigm of a nation under God, possessing land and governed by law. Is there something positive that can be taken from Joshua for thinking about the modern world?

Joshua and Universality

The proposition of Joshua as irredeemably exclusivist may be questioned in a number of ways. As part of the canonical literature of Judaism and Christianity, it can be understood in relation to the other parts of those canons, in creative tension with them. Thus, the prophet Amos challenges any exclusive or triumphalist notion of Israel's election and possession of land by proclaiming that Yahweh, God of Israel, has privileged other nations in the same way as Israel itself (Amos 9.7). A similar position is taken in Deut. 2.2-12, where we read that Yahweh has given territory to Edom and Moab and that their rights of possession set boundaries to the rights of Israel. And numerous Old Testament texts demand an understanding of the nature and vocation of Israel in terms of a divine purpose for the whole world (e.g. Gen. 12.1-3; Isa. 49. 1-6; Deut. 4.6-8). Such texts do not cancel Joshua, but supply a wider context for its reading.

Furthermore, we have observed features of Joshua itself that suggest a qualification of the idea that it is triumphalist and exclusive. These are, first, the strong connection established in the book between Israel's possession of land and the divine ordering of the whole creation (e.g. in Josh.18.1), which is closely related to the symbolic aspects of the representation of events in the book; second, the absorption of Canaanite Rahab and family into the people of Israel, and third, the connection between land-possession, covenant and the keeping of Torah. We have also explored the character of the narrative itself (Chapter 3), which exhibits an ironic tension between the surface meaning (where Israel is given victory over the Canaanites and possesses their land) and a persistent undermining of this by indications that Israel did not in fact take the land. The narrative art of the book also has the effect of putting the integrity of both the land and the people in doubt and showing the precarious situation of Israel in obligation to a covenant which they may never succeed in keeping (Josh. 24.19). All these features point beyond a reading of the book as a narrowly nationalistic account of the rights and privileges of Israel.

These ironies in the discourse of Joshua bear directly on the issue of particularity and universality. Read in the light of Deuteronomy, Joshua arguably participates in a depiction of nationhood that represents a move in the direction of the properly 'political', defined as a transcending of the particular. Political nationhood is understood here in contrast with fundamental kinship identities and ties. The fullest exposition of this, in relation to Deuteronomy, is in Carrière (1997; see the account in McConville 2006: 88-98; see also McBride 1987). Carried on into Joshua, it coheres well with the symbolic and subversive aspects of the book just noted. (Carrière actually thinks the Deuteronomic vision is not continued into the 'historical books', but he offers no analysis of Joshua, such as is given here.)

The apparently strong particularity of Joshua may thus be seen as qualified not just by virtue of external considerations, but by the book itself. In fact, the relationship between particularity and universality in regard to nationhood is in itself complex. In one account of the rise of nations in Europe, Michael Burleigh records post-Reformation attempts to understand the relationship between nationhood and the universality of the Gospel. He quotes Friedrich Schleiermacher, in the context of Pietistic reflections on the subject: 'To serve mankind is noble. But this is possible only when one is convinced of the value of one's own people' (Burleigh 2005: 149; cf. Grosby 2002: 233). We have seen, in the actual use made of Joshua over the centuries, how readily aspirations to embody biblical ideals for nationhood slip into dangerous forms of nationalism. It may be that the powerful language of war deployed in Joshua must bear responsibility for that. Equally, close attention to its discourse has shown that it has the resources to subject nationalistic and triumphalist readings to the most searching criticism.

We return, therefore, to the dilemma posed at the beginning of this chapter: how to sustain a belief in the divine presence in history and also to reject the kind of violence pursued by nations in their own narrow interests? If there is a way through it, it lies in a recognition that the narrative of Yahweh-war in Joshua actually illustrates the dangers of nationalistic triumphalism and contains a sharp challenge to it. If God has been active in history over the centuries since the Bible, this can only be perceived through a lens that sees the story of Israel in Canaan as part of a wider vision for justice and toleration among the nations of the earth.

The Case of Israel–Palestine

One of the remarkable phenomena of the story of nations in the twentieth and twenty-first centuries has been the establishment of the state of Israel. It is inseparable from the larger story of the nations of Christendom that we have briefly reviewed and, ironically, owes a particular debt to that corrupt form of 'Christian' nationhood that was Nazi Germany. It is also a unique application of the biblical narrative of Israel because it claims a direct continuity with it by its adoption of the name 'Israel' itself and by its occupation of the very land (approximately) that was given to ancient Israel in the Old Testament.

The establishment of the modern state of Israel has, therefore, been supported by an extraordinarily compelling narrative. The ancient longing of Jews for the land of their origins, expressed in the words of the Passover service 'Next year in Jerusalem', is readily represented as having been fulfilled in the return of Jews in growing numbers since the nineteenth century, and the establishment of the state of Israel following the Second World War and the holocaust. The conceptual framework for it was available in the Old Testament's account of God's gift of the land to Israel, its occupation of it in the face of opposition from existing inhabitants (in Joshua) and its recurring theme of 'return' following exile. The return, too, is marked by further resistance on the part of existing inhabitants (in Ezra–Nehemiah) and accompanied, in the prophets, by images of the return of Yahweh to Zion together with his victory over nations or their subservience to him (e.g. Isa. 60.10-12; Joel 3; Zech. 1.12-17; 14). This framework was given further shape by Theodor Herzl and the development of Zionism in the late nineteenth century and the special impetus of the revival of Hebrew as a modern language by Eliezer Ben Yehuda. The founders of modern Israel evidently believed in an authority to possess the land that went beyond the protocols of ordinary international relations when they conducted a war of occupation to possess territory that exceeded the limits of what was granted to them by the United Nations, a process and rationale that was extended in 1967, with the occupation of the West Bank. This perceived authority is evidently found in the biblical narratives. The ideas of Zionism were eagerly taken up by many western Christians, who because of influential forms of eschatological interpretation of the Old Testament, saw in the return of Jews to the land a crucial element in the prophesied events of the end times.

In principle, the caveats offered above concerning the possibility of appropriating the biblical narrative of Israel for dangerous and violent forms of nationalism apply identically to the state of Israel. We have seen that the book of Joshua cannot properly be used as a charter for triumphalist and exclusive nationalistic claims. This is partly because of its setting within a wider canon that sets out a vision for the inclusion of all the nations in God's purposes and partly because of the indications we have found within Joshua itself that guard against an exclusivist reading.

In fact, the straightforward adoption of the Israel–Canaan paradigm encounters severe problems. One critique, from within Judaism, comes from Marc Ellis who has lamented the 'Constantinian Judaism' of Zionist nationalism and sees it as locked in a cycle of violence, which he finds (in an echo of Assmann) to be a product of the monotheistic religions (Ellis 2002: 75). His plea for an inclusive polity in modern Israel recalls the points made above about the resources of the Old Testament for the development of democratic and citizenly ideals, though Ellis does not pursue this in the same way.

The existence of non-Jewish peoples in the land for many centuries before the modern influx of Jews is the inevitable and intractable problem for Israel. The Joshua paradigm provides an especially unfortunate typology here, for the Palestinian peoples can readily be cast in the role of Canaanites. As we have seen, this has also happened in other places, but it has particular resonances in the present case. The damaging potential of this typology was shown powerfully by Whitelam (1996), who argued that the biblical portrayal of the nation of Israel and its interpretation by generations of biblical scholars has had the effect of dispossessing the non-Jewish peoples of Palestine of their legitimate claims on the land that had been their home for most of the post-biblical period.

Those peoples, furthermore, have voices of their own. The ancient community of Palestinian Christians has experienced the powerful language of 'Israel' and 'land' most agonizingly because it has severely complicated the use of their own Old Testament Scripture. It is hard to be persuaded of the universalizing potential in a story about 'Israel' taking the land of an indigenous population when a nation called 'Israel' has done that very thing in living memory and present actuality to one's own people. In those circumstances, there is a strong Marcionite temptation. Some, such as the Anglican priest and biblical scholar Naim Ateek, have, however, developed a Palestinian 'liberation theology', which (like the South African version mentioned above) involves a re-reading of the Old Testament with an accent on universality, justice and deliverance. Ateek has addressed the Old Testament story in several works, in which a common theme is the recovery of these inclusive, prophetic Old Testament dynamics (Ateek 1989). Ateek's testimony is particularly powerful because of his personal experience of dispossession and his reading of the Old Testament's theology of land as a Palestinian Christian (e.g. Ateek 2008: 51-66). It is significant that he has confronted his people's situation not by rejecting the Old Testament, but by finding in it (as we have tried to do above) themes that profoundly challenge its use for nationalistic or oppressive purposes. Hermeneutically, his approach is not far from those which have set the 'prophetic' strands of the Old Testament against the 'Deuteronomic' (such as Jewett and Laurence; see above). It is worth just repeating the caveat that this dichotomy is not easy to maintain, and in fact the title of Ateek's 1989 book comes precisely from Deut. 16.20.

There is now a chorus of voices, including Jewish voices, raised in protest against the use of the Old Testament in support of what are seen to be policies of dispossession of peoples and permanent settlement in illegally held land. The approaches advocated include the responsible interpretation of the Old Testament, for example, in the use of prophecy (Chapman 1989; Burge 2003), political theology (Prior 1997) and explorations of alternative Jewish perspectives in relation to justice and land (Ellis 2002; Braverman 2010; Pappé 2004). All oppose the absolute right of one people to possess the land at the expense of the dispossession of another people and promote the co-existence, equal rights and mutual respect of all inhabitants of the land.

From their different points of view, they illustrate the inevitable collision between a straight transfer of the Joshua pattern of total conquest and widely held modern values of tolerance, justice and equality under the law. Braverman illustrates the sharp discrepancy between the simplistic adoption of a conquest pattern and the realities of national, political and religious existence in the modern world. As an American Jew, he traces a line from what he sees as the nationalistic Old Testament to the flagrant human rights abuses of the Israeli state and spends much of his time advocating to American Christian audiences a re-examination of the kind of biblical interpretation that endorses a total conquest pattern in Israel-Palestine. He does this on the basis of commonly held values in modern democratic societies.

Israel–Palestine Today

The issue that is so contentious in Israel-Palestine belongs (among other factors) to the recent history of the interpretation of Joshua. The sense among Jewish and Christian Zionists that 'the land belongs to the Jews' has its roots there. Our study, however, has questioned throughout the validity of the total conquest paradigm. We saw that the book of Joshua itself, when carefully read, undermines it. In a literary-critical approach (as in Chapter 2), one might suppose that a total conquest perspective remains as one voice among others in an uneven history of inner-Old Testament attempts to understand the course of Yahweh's covenant promise to give Israel land. In a more modern literary approach to the book, broadly influenced by Bakhtin (as in Chapter 3 above), the total conquest perspective is sharply called in question because it fails to assert itself as the ultimately authoritative voice in the book. The discussion of genre (Chapter 4) showed that the book is no straight re-telling of history, nor even an ordinary case of a 'conquest account', but that Joshua placed the formative events of Israel in the land within a framework of creation and eschatology in which 'Israel' and land have at most a contingent significance. This is not a telling, or even a patterning, of the 'end of history'. Finally, in theological terms, Joshua could be seen as a 'culture-critique', of which the central topic of the *ḥērem* is an instrument. In a theological reading, the people of Israel is understood as porous (that is, open to 'outsiders') and defined by true worship and covenant faithfulness; and the land, while indispensable to the theological subject-matter of the book, is ill-defined, unstable and impermanent. Finally, in that component of the interpretation of Joshua that is constituted by the history of its use and interpretation, abuses of the notion of God-given nationhood were writ large.

This accumulation of perspectives on Joshua, however, is not to remove it from the sphere of actual history and politics, and thus not to 'spiritualize' it. As was suggested earlier in the present chapter, Joshua is part of a biblical story that has a legacy in many of the values that are commonly shared today in democratic or liberal societies. Rather, the book confronts us with the sharp question as to who or what 'Israel' and 'land' might mean today. The meaning of 'Israel' itself is contested within contemporary Judaism (Ellis); that is, it does not always equate with 'land of Israel' or 'state of Israel'. In the present sub-section, we have begun to use the term Israel-Palestine to designate the area composed of the state of Israel, the West Bank and Gaza and the peoples who co-habit there. This is to recognize that the questions of identity and legitimacy are contested ones.

In Naim Ateek's thinking about justice, he recognizes the need for the further virtue of forgiveness (in a chapter entitled 'From Justice to Forgiveness', Ateek 2008: 178-88). This shows an understanding of the profound relationship between the political realities of justice and peace on one hand, and the realities of the individual's inner life on the other. A powerful contribution to this theme has recently been made by Gopin (2012). His title, *Bridges across an Impossible Divide*, refers to the formidable religious, cultural, historical and spiritual divide between Jews and Arabs in Israel-Palestine. At the same time (intentionally or not), it evokes the 'crossing' of the River Jordan, which we saw to have a symbolic role in Joshua's framing of its radical critique of falsely-based systems. The substance of Gopin's book is the examination of first-person self-analyses by people in the Israel-Palestine conflict who have suffered deeply traumatic personal loss yet have chosen to be peacemakers. A striking aspect of his account is its counter-cultural character, even involving elements of risk (pp. 17-18). One context for such transformative thinking and action is the Parents' Circle, composed of Jews and Arabs who have lost children in the conflict. Gopin recognizes that the hard political realities are inextricably bound to the moral and spiritual decisions that are made in the human heart (pp. 20-26). Connections can be made here to Torah and covenant, where a right orientation moves seamlessly between the private and public spheres (the classic text is Deut. 6.5). Hope for a just and peaceful future in Israel–Palestine is bound to rest on this. The rhetorical flourish of Josh. 24.19 counsels caution; but the peacemakers give a hopeful response.

Conclusion

The history of the use of the book of Joshua illustrates the dangers of its application in simplistic ways. We have seen in earlier chapters how it might be understood in ways that do not lead to xenophobic violence, by paying attention to concepts such as myth, identity and cultural critique and by observing how the book itself contains challenges to its apparent surface-meaning. This means that, in practice, a productive use of the book in specific situations may require the imaginative reading 'against the grain' of the text. In our review of literature in the present chapter, we have seen some ways in which reflection on Joshua can lead to bold thinking about how to relate to situations of conflict. The point is nicely illustrated by Gopin's book. Although it does not set out to be an interpretation of Joshua, it is instructive as an illustration of how a reading of the book might be turned into a reflection on its underlying thrust as a passionate call for liberation from all kinds of tyranny (Brueggemann 2009; cf. Chapter 4 above).

Bibliography

Assmann, Jan. *Moses the Egyptian: The Memory of Egypt in Western Monotheism* (Cambridge, MA: Harvard University Press, 1997).

Ateek, Naim. *A Palestinian Christian Cry for Reconciliation* (Maryknoll, NY: Orbis Books, 2008).

– *Justice and Only Justice: A Palestinian Theology of Liberation* (Maryknoll, NY: Orbis Books, 1989).

Bonhoeffer, Dietrich. *No Rusty Swords* (trans. J. Bowden; New York: Harper & Row, 1956).

Braverman, Mark. *Fatal Embrace: Christians, Jews, and the Search for Peace in the Holy Land* (New York: Beaufort Books, 2010).

Brueggemann, W. *Divine Presence amid Violence: Contextualizing the Book of Joshua* (Milton Keynes: Paternoster/Eugene, OR: Cascade Books, 2009).

– *The Land* (OBT; Philadelphia, PA: Fortress Press, 1977).

Burge, Gary M. *Whose Land? Whose Promise?* (Carlisle: Paternoster, 2003).

Burleigh, Michael. *Earthly Powers: Religion and Politics in Europe from the French Revolution to the Great War* (London: HarperCollins, 2005).

– *Sacred Causes: Religion and Politics from the European Dictators to Al Qaeda* (London: HarperCollins, 2006).

Burnside, Jonathan. *God, Justice and Society: Aspects of Law and Legality in the Bible* (Oxford: Oxford University Press, 2011).

Carrière, J.-M. *La théorie du politique dans le Deutéronome* (ÖBS, 18; Frankfurt: Peter Lang, 1997).

Chapman, Colin. *Whose Promised Land?* (Lion: Tring, revised edn, 1989).

Crüsemann, Frank D. *The Torah: Theology and Social History of Old Testament Law* (Minneapolis, MN: Fortress Press, 1996).

Earl, Douglas S. *Reading Joshua as Christian Scripture* (JTISup, 2; Winona Lake, IN: Eisenbrauns, 2010).

Ellis, Marc. *Israel and Palestine: Out of the Ashes. The Search for Jewish Identity in the Twenty-First Century* (London and Sterling, VA: Pluto Press, 2002).

Gopin, Marc. *Bridges across an Impossible Divide: The Inner Lives of Arab and Jewish Peacemakers* (Oxford: Oxford University Press, 2012).

Grosby, Steven. *Biblical Ideas of Nationality Ancient and Modern* (Winona Lake, IN; Eisenbrauns, 2002).

Hitchens, Christopher. *God Is Not Great* (London: Atlantic Books, 2007).

Jenkins, Philip. *Laying Down the Sword: Why We Can't Ignore the Bible's Violent Verses* (New York: HarperOne, 2011).

Jewett, Robert, and John Shelton Laurence, *Captain America and the Crusade against Evil* (Grand Rapids, MI: Eerdmans, 2003).

McBride, S.D. 'Polity of the Covenant People: The Book of Deuteronomy', *Interpretation* 41 (1987), pp. 229-44.

McConville, J.G. *God and Earthly Power* (London: T. & T. Clark International, 2006).

O'Donovan, Oliver. *Desire of the Nations: Rediscovering the Roots of Political Theology* (Cambridge: Cambridge University Press, 1996).

Pappé, Ilan. *A History of Modern Palestine: One Land, Two Peoples* (Cambridge: Cambridge University Press, 2004).

Porter, Jean. *Natural and Divine Law: Reclaiming the Tradition for Christian Ethics* (Grand Rapids, MI: Eerdmans, 1999).

Prior, Michael. *The Bible and Colonialism: A Moral Critique* (The Biblical Seminar, 48; Sheffield: Sheffield Academic Press, 1997).

Schwartz, Regina. *The Curse of Cain: The Violent Legacy of Monotheism* (Chicago and London; University of Chicago Press, 1997).

Smith, A.D. *Chosen Peoples* (Oxford and New York: Oxford University Press, 2003).

Taylor, Charles. *A Secular Age* (Cambridge, MA and London: Belknap Press of Harvard University Press, 2007).

Whitelam, Keith. *The Invention of Ancient Israel: The Silencing of Palestinian History* (London: Routledge, 1996).

INDEX OF AUTHORS

INDEX OF SUBJECTS